JOHN MILTON

Paradise Lost: Books III–IV

£1-95

THE CAMBRIDGE MILTON FOR SCHOOLS AND COLLEGES

GENERAL EDITOR: J. B. BROADBENT

Already published:

John Milton: introductions, edited by John Broadbent

Odes, Pastorals, Masques, edited by
David Aers, John Broadbent, Winifred Maynard,
Peter Mendes, and Lorna Sage

Paradise Lost: introduction, John Broadbent

Paradise Lost: books I–II, edited by John Broadbent

Paradise Lost: books V–VI, edited by
Robert Hodge and Isabel MacCaffrey

Paradise Lost: books VII–VIII, edited by
David Aers and Mary Ann Radzinowicz

Paradise Lost: books IX–X, edited by J. Martin Evans

Paradise Lost: books XI–XII, edited by
Michael Hollington with Lawrence Wilkinson

Samson Agonistes, Sonnets &c, edited by John Broadbent and Robert
Hodge (with translations of selected Latin and Italian poetry)

JOHN MILTON

Paradise Lost: Books III–IV

Edited by
LOIS POTTER
University of Leicester

JOHN BROADBENT
University of East Anglia, Norwich

io compresi
me sormontar di sopr'a mia virtute;
e di novella vista mia raccesi
tale, che nulla luce è tanto mera,
che li occhi miei non si fosser difesi.
E vidi lume in forma di rivera
fulvido di fulgore, intra due rive
dipinte di mirabil primavera.

Quelli ch'anticamente poetaro
l'età dell'oro e suo stato felice,
forse in Parnaso esto loco sognaro.
Qui fu innocente l'umana radice;
qui primavera sempre ed ogni frutto;
nettare è questo di che ciascun dice.

DANTE ALIGHIERI *Paradiso* xxx   *Purgatorio* xxviii c. 1310

And the end of all our exploring
Will be to arrive where we started
And know the place for the first time.
Through the unknown, remembered gate
When the last of earth left to discover
Is that which was the beginning...
And the children in the apple-tree
Not known, because not looked for
But heard, half-heard, in the stillness.

T. S. ELIOT *Little Gidding* Faber 1942

Cambridge University Press

CAMBRIDGE

LONDON   NEW YORK   NEW ROCHELLE

MELBOURNE   SYDNEY

Published by the Press Syndicate of the University of Cambridge
The Pitt Building, Trumpington Street, Cambridge CB2 1RP
32 East 57th Street, New York, NY 10022, USA
296 Beaconsfield Parade, Middle Park, Melbourne 3206, Australia

First published 1976
Reprinted 1980 (twice) 1981

Printed in Great Britain at the
University Press, Cambridge

Library of Congress Cataloguing in Publication Data
Milton, John, 1608–1674
Paradise Lost: books III–IV.
(The Cambridge Milton for schools and colleges)
I. Potter, Lois.   II. Broadbent, John Barclay.   III. Title.
IV. Series.
PR3560.P6 1976 821'.4 75–36681
ISBN 0 521 21150 6

Acknowledgement

The cover illustrations are from stone statues of Adam and Eve carved c. 1490 by Tilman Riemenschneider for a portal of the Marienkapelle (church of Notre Dame) in Würzburg, northern Bavaria, and now in the Mainfränkisches Museum, Würzburg (and reproduced here with permission of the Museum). This work was done in the transition from Gothic to renaissance; it seems astoundingly 'Miltonic' in the play of sympathy with grandeur; and in their own right these representations of Adam and Eve are perhaps the greatest in the world. Würzburg is worth a pilgrimage; so is Bamberg, 70 km to the east, which has a charming and rather childlike Adam and Eve.

Contents

The editors

Books III and IV have been edited independently by:

Book III

LOIS POTTER Bryn Mawr, Cambridge, Leicester. Author of *A preface to Milton*. She has also written on Elizabethan drama and Robin Hood.

Book IV

JOHN BROADBENT Edinburgh, Cambridge, East Anglia. Author of *Poetic love*; *Some graver subject: an essay on PL* and other works on Milton, and general editor of this series; editor of Smart's *Song to David* and of an anthology *Poets of the 19c*. Professor Broadbent is married to a social worker.

Preface to the Cambridge Milton

We have also considered him as a poet, and such he was, if ever human nature could boast it had produced one...in expounding him we have therefore always given, as well as we were enabled, a poetic sense...for a poem, such a one as this especially, is not to be read, and construed, as an Act of Parliament, or a mathematical dissertation: the things of the spirit are spiritually discerned.

JONATHAN RICHARDSON father and son *Explanatory notes and remarks on Paradise Lost* 1734

This volume is part of the Cambridge Milton series. It can be used independently but we assume that you refer as appropriate to two other volumes in particular:

John Milton: introductions. A collaborative volume listed under the general editor's name. For Milton's life, times, ideas; music, visual arts, science, the Bible in relation to his poetry; a long essay on *Milton in literary history* and *General introduction to the early poems.*

Paradise Lost: introduction. J. B. Broadbent. General introduction to the poem as a whole with chapters on myth and ritual; epic; history of publication; ideology; structures; allusion; language; syntax; rhetoric; minor components of epic; similes; rhythm; style. This volume also contains a full list of resources (books, art, music etc.); a chronology of the Bible and biblical writings, epics, and other versions of the material of *PL* (this section constitutes a list of materials for projects); and a table of the contents of *PL* with cross-references.

The series will supersede A. W. Verity's Pitt Press edition of Milton's poetry published from Cambridge 1891 *et seq.* It is designed for use by the individual student, and the class, and the teacher, in schools and colleges, from about the beginning of the sixth form to the end of the first postgraduate year in England. Introductions and notes aim to provide enough material for the reader to work on for himself, but nothing of a professionally academic kind. We hope that if any volume of text is prescribed for examination, some of its contents will not be set, but left for the student to explore at will.

Examining, teaching, study

Milton's poems need more annotation to achieve a given degree of comprehension and pleasure than most others. Shakespeare, Donne, Blake, Yeats all demand annotation; but they arouse interest more immediately than Milton does, and so motivate study. This difficulty does not lie in the idleness of the reader or his ignorance: it was felt by Dr Johnson (admittedly a slothful man, but also a learned one and himself an editor). *PL* was one of the first English poems to be annotated. In 1695, twenty-one years after Milton died, Patrick Hume published his *Annotations... Wherein the Texts of Sacred Writ Relating to the Poem, are Quoted; The Parallel Places and Imitations of the Most Excellent Homer and Virgil, Cited and Compared; All the Obscure Parts Render'd in Phrases More Familiar; The Old and Obsolete Words, with Their Originals, Explain'd and Made Easie...* As editors we are all guilty, like Hume, of answering the wrong questions. As examiners, we're guilty of asking them. Milton's poetry is worth using in education because it is difficult; but we have to attend to the right kind of difficulty. In *PL* the serious difficulties are not the surface obscurities of

> nor to which transform'd
> *Ammonian Jove*, or *Capitoline* was seen,
> Hee with *Olympias*, this with her who bore
> *Scipio* the highth of *Rome*.   IX 507

They are the grave issues of sin, death, 'all our woe', grace, the use of beauty and strength, 'conjugal love'. Those are also the interesting things. But they tend to get left out of editions, and exam papers, because they are more suitable for discussion than for notes and tests. It's the same with Milton's earlier poems. *Arcades* is a little masque he wrote for the Countess of Derby and her family. It has a song that ends

> Though Syrinx your Pan's mistress were,
> Yet Syrinx well might wait on her.
> > Such a rural queen
> All Arcadia hath not seen.

In 1969 one of the public examining boards in England asked for 'a brief explanatory note' on those lines. In a way, the answer is simple if indelicate: Pan tried to rape Syrinx so she jumped into a river and turned into a reed. But whatever does it mean in the context? Can the Countess of Derby have suffered such an adventure? Editors are helpless. Verity quotes Tennyson on the preterite subjunctive but does not elucidate; neither, of recent editions, does the most academically distinguished, nor the most school-aimed. I suppose we should be discussing the relationship between goat-god and woman, river and music; that is really difficult.

The best elementary exam on *PL* that I have seen was set in the summer of 1968 on *PL* iv and ix. It asked for either an essay, or a series of shorter answers on a printed passage: so two sorts of candidate were each given a decent chance to show their best. The essay topic was large yet crucial: in effect, did Adam and Eve *have* to fall? No nonsense about Satan's 'character' dragged in from the Shakespeare paper, or invitations to be romantic about Milton's soul. The printed passage was from Satan's soliloquy on arriving in paradise, and the candidates were told so. Four questions directed the candidate to specific locales – 'What do the phraseology and form of these four lines tell you about Satan's own nature?' for instance. The fifth asked for the passage to be related to its parallel in Book ix. In short, the candidates' memory and attention were being helped; but they were being asked seriously difficult questions.

Here are some suggestions for overcoming the difficulties of Milton's poetry in spite of the editor:

Editing. Never learn footnotes. On the contrary, annotate parts of the text for yourself. You will find the answers to most problems in *Brewer's dictionary of phrase and fable* and the *Shorter Oxford English dictionary*; occasionally you may need a classical dictionary (such as Keats learned out of), and a handbook to English and European literature (eg the Penguin *Companions to literature*), and a concordance to the Bible.

Performance. Study Milton's poetry out loud to elicit its variousness:

And cast the dark foundations deep	*Nativity* 123
Trip the pert fairies and the dapper elves	*Comus* 118
When that comes think not thou to find me slack	*PR* III 398

To study aloud means reading aloud to understand; alone and together; against music, chanting if you like. It includes acting the poetry. Don't try to act, say, the Muses and Old Camus in *Lycidas*; but express in a physical way (especially passively) some of the qualities or states of existence that occur in the poem: eg look for the words applied to Lycidas's corpse (float, welter, hurled) and enact them.

Performance may include other kinds of manipulation. Consider how much we use other poetry – hymns, liturgy, pop songs, metaphors, riddles, ritualistic puns and fantasies. Extend the material from 'poetry' to include the sort of thing that Milton's poetry contains – language, mythology, theology, geography – and it becomes clear that we could *use* Milton's poetry in all sorts of ways, if we were not afraid. The advantage of great poetry is that you can criticize it: it stands up to you, and so gives you an idea, gradually, of what is durable and what disposable, or likely to rot. But another advantage of great poetry is that you can do many things with it. Other poets are not afraid to manipulate:

The sun and the moon shall be dark, and the stars shall withdraw their
shining.   *Joel* ii 10

> O dark, dark, dark, amid the blaze of noon,
> Irrecoverably dark, total eclipse
> Without all hope of day   *Samson* 80

O dark dark dark. They all go into the dark
The vacant interstellar spaces, the vacant into the vacant.
                                        T. S. ELIOT *East Coker* 1940 Faber

There Milton manipulates the Bible, Eliot manipulates Milton. We could probably enrich our own experience of the *Samson* passage better than this through music or paint – as Handel and Rembrandt did. Try representing in a non-verbal medium a sun which is as silent as an invisible moon.

Analysis. As you perform and manipulate the work, much of what it is about will emerge. Now start to analyse it more consciously. The best way to do this at first is on the fairly large scale of shape and structure.

What is the shape of this poem? Where are the soft pastoral

parts, and where the strident military ones? If I shut my eyes and transform my image of the poem into colours, or music, a journey, a body, a life, what is it like? I notice in the middle of *Lycidas* a knot of darkness, clanging metal, infection, greed, blows. Can I refine my account, arrange it in terms of a single metaphor? What are those things doing in the poem anyway? How do they relate to the flatness at the very end, the spread-out hills, the distant sea, the set sun?

Then, what features in the poem set up structures of their own? This often happens with items that are repeated. The sun in *Lycidas* recurs, along with other stars, with planets, with the moon, and with the concepts of the year, time, ripeness and so on; it seems to oppose the weltering waves.

Comprehension. Before interpreting *Lycidas*, though, we have to check our comprehension of its details: eg why does Phoebus in line 77 rank as part of the star structure? I put this late in the process because most of our small-scale difficulties will be solved as we perform and analyse the poetry. To put it in editorial terms, an inch of introduction is worth a yard of footnote.

Examiners have a fondness for those parts of Milton's work which (like the arguments in Pandemonium) have a paraphrasable content. Unfortunately, Milton is practically unparaphrasable, especially in such contexts. His language contains little in the way of metaphors to be unpacked. It is impregnable, for it works in large blocks of idiosyncratic syntax. Soon after you start to analyse the argument you find you have forgotten where it began. Milton's poetry does need a special kind of comprehension; but it is to be tested not by trying to 'translate' or 'construe' Milton; but by acquiring a sense of what you need to know. When you have grasped, by performance, and by structural analysis, what a poem or passage is about, look closely at the words which don't fit your understanding. In *Lycidas* you don't know where Mona, Bellerus, Namancos are. Look them up and you will find they are Anglesey, Land's End and so on. But these identities don't matter. What matters is, first, that Milton should have clad them in old names and mythology; and, second, that they are all western: they ring the sea where Lycidas drowned, and ring the sunset. In short, it is more important to register quality than learn genealogy.

How, though, can you recognize your need for knowledge in the case of an isolated word? Quite often, you can't. A lot of our ignorance has to *wait* to be informed, gradually, often accidentally.

But you can avoid some traps by, again, attending to the verse and the structure, eg:

Russet lawns and fallows grey   *L'allegro* 71

The colours enclose the landscape, so obviously they are important. Try to visualize the line and you will at once feel the need for help.

Peace, brother, be not over-exquisite
To cast the fashion of uncertain evils   *Comus* 359

As often in Shakespeare, you can't put any expression into the lines until you have found out what the words mean.

Attention

The reader of Milton must be always up on duty: he is surrounded with sense, it rises in every line, every word is to the purpose; there are no lazy intervals; all has been considered, and demands, and merits observation. Even in the best writers you sometimes find words and sentences which hang on so loosely you may blow 'em off; Milton's are all substance and weight. If this be called obscurity, let it be remembered that it is such an obscurity as is a compliment to the reader; not that vicious obscurity which proceeds from a muddled head.

Coleridge copied that into his commonplace book out of the *Explanatory notes on PL* of 1734 by Jonathan Richardson, the painter, and his son. Consider what the parallel in your ordinary life might be of the kind of attention you could give to Milton.

This edition of Milton

The texts are based on the latest editions published in his lifetime: ie chiefly *Poems of Mr John Milton, both English and Latin* (the earlier poems) 1645; and the second edition of *PL* 1674. But the text has no authority as such.

The spelling has been modernized (except where it would completely alter pronunciation, eg *anow* has been changed to *enow* but not to *enough*).

Stress marks (′) have been added where Milton seems to have intended a stress unusual for us, eg *óbscene*. Grave accents (`) have been added to indicate voiced syllables in such cases as *blessèd* and in unfamiliar names, eg *Atè*. Milton distinguished between stressed and unstressed forms of *hee, he, their, thir*, etc. These have all been reduced to their normal modern forms.

Milton showed much elision of *e*'s, eg 'th'obscene dread of Moab's sons', 'th'heavens'. These have been omitted too because the elision comes more naturally if we read it with our usual neutral *e* sounds in such cases, than if we try to say *thóbscene* or *theavens*.

On the other hand, Milton's punctuation has been left almost untouched. It is not the same as ours, but you soon get used to it, and to tamper would alter the rhythm. In particular, modern punctuation would interrupt the flow of ideas. For example, a passage about Eve's hair:

> She as a veil down to the slender waist
> Her unadornèd golden tresses wore
> Dishevelled, but in wanton ringlets waved
> As the vine curls her tendrils, which implied
> Subjection, but required with gentle sway,
> And by her yielded, by him best received,
> Yielded with coy submission, modest pride,
> And sweet reluctant amorous delay.   *PL* IV 304

Pause at each punctuation mark. Pause at all awkward line-changes, eg 'implied/Subjection' puts a pause equal to a whole stress between the lines. Let all neutral vowels stay neutral, eg *tendrils*, *required*, *yielded*. Run over unstressed words as in ordinary speech, eg 'She as a veil' is nearly elided as 'She's a veil'; but give all stressed syllables their full value. Don't be officious with the syntax: its sense is impressionistic rather than logical. The words implied–required–yielded–received are set in a pattern which represents a relationship, not a grammar: Eve's hair implies subjection; Adam requires that subjection of her, gently; she does actually yield – also perhaps gently; and he receives it, takes it back again – and then she goes on yielding it, her yielding and her reluctance to yield both an expression of love, her *delay* the rhyming answer to his *sway* (= power). It is not a sentence but a dance.

Milton's meanings are often etymological, eg *dishevelled* does not mean unkempt but let down without coiffure; *reluctant* does not mean unwilling but resistant; these meanings will emerge more easily if the words are dwelt on and given their full syllabic value – *dis-chevelled*, *re-luctant*. Reading Hopkins helps because he uses words etymologically. But do not elocute. Actors' voices have a particularly bad effect on Milton because his language is hardly ever beautiful or emotive – it is stiff and thoughtful, or colloquial and definite:

The leaf was darkish, and had prickles on it,
But in another country, as he said,
Bore a bright golden flower, but not in this soil.

Comus 631

        but all sat mute,
Pondering the danger with deep thoughts; and each
In other's countenance read his own dismay
Astonished.

PL II 420

In the second passage there, one might emphasize the emotions of dismay and astonishment; but as a matter of fact, *astonished* means *dismayed*; and what matters is the shape, the structure of the lines; it is that, not expressiveness, which represents the fallen angels' bafflement. The structure runs: an angel – another angel – own dismay – more dismay. It is better to read with an eye to semantics than to histrionics; and to read as Milton did (with a provincial accent, rather harshly, with something of a sarcastic note, rolling his *r*'s) than with elegance.

In the face of the syllabus – heavy for many subjects – 'adventures of ideas' in wider fields, and the time-consuming operations of developing independence of thought. . .will be undertaken 'at risk'.

> Report of the Welsh Committee of the Schools Council, in Schools Council Working Paper 20, *Sixth-form examining methods*, HMSO 1968.

This edition assumes that risk.

Note about this volume

PL III is about heaven, and the solar system; IV is about paradise. Those are the names we use; but heaven is sometimes called paradise, as in the first quotation from Dante on the title-page. Paradise is sometimes called, to distinguish it, the earthly paradise, or the Garden of Eden (Eden being the district it lies in). The title-page's second extract from Dante is about the earthly paradise: the poet sees it as he emerges from his tour of purgatory. The extract from Eliot there puts them together: the end and the beginning are images of each other. To adapt a diagram from Harry Levin *The myth of the Golden Age in the renaissance* Faber 1970:

Heaven	celestial	eternal	city	millenarian/ religious
Paradise of Eden	terrestrial/ celestial	past	garden	primitivistic
Arcadia	terrestrial	past	sheepwalks, forest	primitivistic
Utopia	terrestrial	future	city	millenarian/ secular

J.B.B.

Introduction to Book III

III 1–55 *Invocation*

Light

At the beginning of Book I Milton had prayed, 'What in me is dark Illumine' (22–3); in the invocation to Book VII he describes himself 'In darkness, and with dangers compassed round' (27). But notice that the address to light is echoed in the intervening books: in Satan's soliloquy in IV and the descriptions of the coming of morning at the beginning of V and VI.

What sort of light is Milton addressing? Not, like Satan later, the sun. Sun-worship had always been a particularly serious rival to Christianity because in many ways it was similar: sunset and sunrise are a daily cycle of death and resurrection. In *Man and the sun* by Jacquetta Hawkes 1962 you can read two hymns to the sun, one by the Pharaoh Ahknaton and one by the Emperor Julian ('the Apostate') who was trying to find a replacement for Christianity as the official religion of the Roman Empire. Christ's halo and chariot, in early representations, make him look like some sort of sun god.

Worship of the sun was bound up with belief in its all-important position in the cosmos. This may be why medieval orthodoxy adopted the cosmology of Aristotle, in which the sun was just one of several planets and the universe was moved *from the outside* by a force (the First Mover, or God) which turned all the spheres at once. An alternative view was that of Pythagoras and Plato, who believed that the universe was moved *from within* by a central fire which might be identified with the sun and thus become an object of worship. From the time of Copernicus onward, such a belief again became possible and, in the work of Kepler (1571–1630), absolutely central.

In Kepler's universe, all mystic attributes and physical powers are centralized in the sun, and the First Mover is returned to the focal position where he belongs. The visible universe is the symbol and 'signature' of the Holy Trinity: the sun represents the Father, the sphere of the fixed stars the Son, the invisible forces which, emanating from the Father, act through interstellar space, represent the Holy Ghost...The shifting of the First Mover from the periphery of the universe into the physical body of the sun, symbol of the God head, prepared the way to the concept of a gravitational force, symbol of the Holy Ghost, which controls the planets. Thus a purely mystical inspiration was the root out of which the first rational theory of the dynamics of the universe developed, based on the secular trinity of Kepler's laws.

ARTHUR KOESTLER The sleepwalkers Penguin 1959

Poets were aware of the danger of falling into this kind of pagan mysticism:

> Thou lamp of God, and spacious world's vast light,
> Of thee how shall I sing? of thee how write?
>   For here I find the danger is,
>   With bards of old, the way to miss.
> Of thee a God they strangely wond'ring made,
> And to thy fire devoutly homage paid.

THOMAS TRAHERNE Hexameron 'fourth day', before 1674

The sun-worshippers thought of light as coming from the sun, but in *Genesis* i it seems the other way round: light is created on the first day, the sun only on the fourth. Either way, the relation between light and the sun provided a rich analogy with the relationship between the first and second persons of the trinity. For English writers there was an added attraction in the easiness of the pun on sun and Son: see, eg, Herbert's *The Sonne* and Donne's *Good Friday* and *Hymn to God the Father*. We can *see* the sun, but we see *by means of* light. Similarly, God is invisible and unknowable except when he takes the form of divine radiance embodied in the Son. These are some of the speculations which lie behind the first dozen lines of the invocation.

So it seems probable that Milton is primarily addressing the true Muse of his poem who, as Broadbent says (introduction to *PL* I in this series), 'is really God himself, as Logos or creating Word'. But 'light' carries many meanings in Book III, as you can see from the various kinds of 'darkness' with which it is contrasted:

Light	*Darkness*
creation	chaos
heaven	hell
the sun	night
sight	blindness
knowledge	ignorance
divine grace	hardening of the heart

Light	Darkness
glory (the state of the blessed)	mortality
inspiration (poetic and prophetic)	spiritual blindness
conscience	clouded reason of fallen man

One might also add:

the rational, conscious, masculine principle	the antithetical feminine principle

That is, the *yin* and the *yang*.

The contrast between these two principles is built into our whole way of thinking. For instance, in most languages 'sun' is masculine and 'earth' is feminine. Milton also follows tradition in regarding the sun and moon as

> Communicating male and female light,
> Which two great sexes animate the world.   VIII 150

This sun–moon relationship reminds us that darkness generally contains some reflection of light; it may even try to imitate it, as when 'Satan himself is transformed into an angel of light' (*II Corinthians* xi) for his encounter with Uriel. Theologically speaking, God contains everything in himself, darkness as well as light: he is 'dark with excessive bright' (III 380) because he cannot be looked on directly. So contrast gives way to paradox. Milton's own *literal* darkness is illuminated by *spiritual* light, whereas Uriel, 'The sharpest sighted spirit of all in heaven' (III 691), can't detect Satan in his disguise.

Orpheus and the underworld journey

The myth of Orpheus was a favourite one with Milton (see *PL: introduction* 81). Not only was its hero a prototype of the poet-prophet, loved by the gods but misunderstood by his fellow-men (he died the victim of a frenzied mob), he was also traditionally associated with a mystic cult which still had considerable attraction for the renaissance. He was supposed to have said, for instance, that love was blind (as in pictures of Cupid) because it was above and beyond the intellect; see the chapter on 'Orpheus in praise of blind love' in Edgar Wind's *Pagan mysteries in the renaissance* 1967. As one who had made a journey to the underworld and returned safely, he could also be compared with Christ, though Christ, of course, *had* succeeded in redeeming his bride, the Christian church. Orpheus's failure to rescue Eurydice, because he disobeyed Pluto's command and looked back on her before he reached the surface, lent itself to a number of moralistic interpretations: the hero should conquer his own feelings, the hero should keep his eyes fixed on heaven instead of this world, etc. Does this mean that Orpheus, for Milton, is more of a warning than a model?

In Monteverdi's opera *Orfeo* 1607 the hero is accompanied as far as the gates of hell by a female personification of hope. She can go no farther after this because – as she says, quoting Dante – those who enter hell must 'abandon all hope'. However, most heroes who make an underworld journey have a female helper: Odysseus relies on Athene throughout his travels and on Circe's directions for his visit to hades; Aeneas is protected by his mother Venus and advised by the Sibyl. Though Satan's journey is often compared to those of the classical epic heroes, it is hard to see Sin as a protectress; he has to go it alone. But Milton does have a female guide on his metaphorical journey, though she only appears intermittently and does not receive her name – Urania – until Book VII. Like Circe and the Sibyl she shows him the way to hell; like Dante's Beatrice she makes it possible for him to breathe the air of heaven. She is the only female presence in what is otherwise a remarkably masculine concept of the spiritual world. But if Milton's Muse is the Logos, what is Urania? The same concept, but in its maternal, protective, female aspect? And why?

Blindness

Metaphorically, Milton has been making a journey from hell to heaven with the aid of a heavenly muse, but there is another level on which he is more like the blind king of *Oedipus at Colonus* being guided by his daughter Antigone. The repetition of 'revisit' (III 13, 21, 23) emphasizes the paradox – he revisits light, but light does not revisit him. Singing *about* eternal night becomes singing *in* eternal night. Or whistling in the dark?

'I see' often means 'I understand'. This is one of many examples of how we associate sight and knowledge. Milton says that his blindness has cut him off from human society, from human knowledge, and even, 'at one entrance' (III 50), from wisdom, which is the knowledge of God. The belief that nature was a book, comparable to the scriptures, from which man could deduce the existence of God goes back to the Bible: 'The heavens declare the glory of God: and the firmament sheweth his handiwork' (*Psalm* xix 1). There was also a separate tradition which starts with Plato's *Symposium*: since it was difficult for man to contemplate abstract goodness and beauty, he should work up to it by contemplating specific examples of goodness and beauty in the world around him. The best expression of this idea in Christian neo-platonism (notice how similar the images are to Milton's) is found in Spenser's *Hymn of heavenly beauty* 1596. After exhorting his reader to read the beauty of God's works 'as in a brazen book', he passes on to the next stage of meditation, which seems to reverse the process:

> Thence gathering plumes of perfect speculation,
> To imp the wings of thy high flying mind,
> Mount up aloft, through heavenly contemplation,
> From this dark world, whose damps the soul do blind,
> And, like the native brood of eagle's kind,
> On that bright sun of glory fix thine eyes,
> Cleared from gross mists of frail infirmities.

The sight of this world, at first a help, is later regarded as a hindrance to full knowledge of God.

Perhaps this is why there are so many legends of blind poets and prophets: do we instinctively feel that it's impossible for a man to have both kinds of knowledge at once? There seem to be two versions of the 'blind bard' concept.

1. *Punitive*. Most of the examples that Milton cites in III 35–6 are of men struck blind by the gods as a punishment for some crime. Thamyris presumed to challenge the Muses to a singing contest; Phineus revealed the secrets of the gods; Tiresias was the victim of Juno's revenge because he took Jupiter's side in an argument. Bellerophon, to whom Milton refers in VII 17–20, attempted to fly to Olympus on his winged horse Pegasus (a traditional symbol of poetic inspiration) and was punished by being thrown down to earth where he spent the rest of his life blind and alone. Why do you think Milton – whose political enemies had claimed that his blindness was God's judgment on him, and who knew that his poetic ambition was daring in every way – keeps invoking such frightening precedents?

2. *Compensatory*. According to Ovid (*Metamorphoses* III), Tiresias was granted long life and the gift of prophecy by Jupiter to make up for Juno's cursing him with blindness; we like to believe that all misfortunes have their compensations. Egyptian hieroglyphics have preserved a similar legend in the symbol for

the eye of Horus the sun god, which is made up of smaller hieroglyphs representing the fractions used in calculating:

In an ancient myth, no doubt representing the fight between day and night, good and evil, the evil god Seth attacked and tore to pieces the eye of Horus. Thoth, the god of learning, reason and justice, put the pieces together again to make the 'sound eye of Horus'. Possibly the fragmenting and mending of the sun-eye was suggested by partial loss of the sun in eclipses.

R. L. GREGORY The intelligent eye Weidenfeld & Nicolson 1970

Homer is always thought of as blind but in fact his name is said to derive from a Greek word meaning eyes (this is why Milton calls him by his surname Maeonides in III 35). In *The Odyssey* he described a typical example of compensatory blindness:

The herald came near, bringing with him the excellent singer whom the Muse had loved greatly, and gave him both good and evil. She reft him of his eyes, but she gave him the sweet singing art.

trans. Lattimore 1965

Similar things were said about Milton's contemporary, Galileo, who was a poet as well as an astronomer and who went blind in his old age. And Andrew Marvell concluded his dedicatory verses to the 1674 edition of *PL*:

> Just heaven thee like Tiresias to requite
> Rewards with prophecy thy loss of sight.

Any one who has common sense will remember that the bewilderments of the eyes are of two kinds, and arise from two causes, either from coming out of the light or from going into the light, which is true of the mind's eye, quite as much as of the bodily eye; and he who remembers this when he sees any one whose vision is perplexed and weak, will not be too ready to laugh; he will first ask whether that soul of man has come out of the brighter life, and is unable to see because unaccustomed to the dark, or having turned from darkness to the day is dazzled by excess of light.

PLATO Republic trans. Jowett

III 56–134   *God foresees the fall*

Argument. God sitting on his throne sees Satan flying towards this world, then newly created; shows him to the Son who sat at his right hand; foretells the success of Satan in perverting mankind; clears his own justice and wisdom from all imputation, having created man free and able enough to have withstood his tempter; yet declares his purpose of grace towards him, in regard he fell not of his own malice, as did Satan, but by him seduced.

God

Notice that we do not *see* God; rather, we are made to see through his eyes (compare Milton's introduction of Satan 1 56–60 looking around 'as far as angels ken'). The panoramic view is imitated from Virgil:

Now a new day threw open the halls of almighty Olympus,
And a council was called by the Father of heaven, the ruler of mankind,
To meet in his sky palace where, from the heights, he surveyed
All earth, the Trojan encampment, and the peoples of Latium.
Aeneid x trans. C. Day Lewis, Oxford U.P. 1952

and Tasso:

When God Almighty from his lofty throne,
  Set in those parts of heaven that purest are,
As far above the clear stars every one,
  As it is hence up to the highest star,
Look'd down, and all at once this world beheld,
Each land, each city, country, town and field.
Jerusalem delivered 1 trans. Fairfax 1600

But the cinematic technique is Milton's own. Having just told us that he can see nothing, he now adopts the viewpoint of a God who sees all things simultaneously; he describes them, however, consecutively – heaven, earth, 'Hell and the gulf between', Satan – in order of their distance from the infinite goodness at the centre of the vision. Satan has been the centre of our interest during his terrifying journey through Chaos but now the camera pulls back, leaving him a tiny figure at the edge of the picture. From now on, we should see him – and everything else – through God's eyes.

But do we? Most readers think not, for two reasons.

1. *Artistic.* Milton presents himself throughout as a mouthpiece for God, but in practice this makes God look like a mouthpiece for Milton. He felt quite strongly that God, in the Bible, had a personality that could be described in human terms. It said, for example: 'It repented the Lord that he had made man, and it grieved him at his heart' (*Genesis* vi 6), 'he rested, and was refreshed' (*Exodus* xxxi 17), even that he 'feared the wrath of the enemy' (*Deuteronomy* xxxii 27). Some commentators had tried to take these expressions allegorically; Milton had no patience with this approach:

In a word, God either is, or is not, such as he represents himself to be. If he be really such, why should we think otherwise of him? If he be not such, on what authority do we say what God has not said? If it be his will that we should thus think of him, why does our imagination wander into some other conception? Why should we hesitate to conceive God according to what he has not hesitated to declare explicitly respecting himself? *De doctrina christiana* I. 2 'Of God'

He was particularly struck by the harshness and scorn sometimes shown by God, which he had used as justification for his own style in political and religious controversy.

And this I shall easily aver, though it may seem a hard saying, that the Spirit of God, who is purity itself, when he would rebuke any fault severely, or but relate things done or said with indignation by others, abstains not from some words not civil at other times to be spoken.
Apology for Smectymnuus 1642

The unpopularity of Milton's God with the average reader seems to me the result of his having not too little personality but too much – too much, in particular, of Milton's personality. They share the same sarcastic sense of humour and fondness for puns (eg 'transports' in God's opening speech III 80–1), the same brisk, no-nonsense style, the same tendency to look down on mankind in more than a literal sense. Being good, they are honest; being honest, they *say* that they are good. Naturally this makes us want to disagree. Why are we more ready to sympathize with a bad man who says he is bad than with a good man who says he is good? Perhaps this problem has more to do with our own psychology than with Milton's artistry.

2. *Theological.* What Milton had to do in *PL* was to reconcile three different aspects of the Judeo-Christian God: (*a*) *the God of love* – an embodiment of all that man can imagine as best in himself, merciful, forgiving, infinitely understanding; (*b*) *the God of justice* – an absolute standard of truth; (*c*) *the creator of the world* – the ultimate source of responsibility for man and his fate, good or bad.

(*a*) and (*b*) are not really reconcilable at all; most people who believe in God emphasize one at the expense of the other. Some allegorists (eg Giles Fletcher in *Christ's victory and triumph in heaven* 1610) get round the problem by presenting a debate between personifications of Justice and Mercy while God listens, serenely above the battle.

(*a*) and (*c*), taken together, require an act of faith: 'God's plan for the world is good, even though it may not seem so at the moment.' Otherwise the result is atheism: 'The world is full of evil, therefore it cannot be the work of a loving God.'

(*b*) and (*c*) can only be reconciled by accepting some form of

17

predestination, which, of course, is hardly reconcilable with (*a*) except by an act of faith. It was precisely this problem which the humanist Erasmus raised at the beginning of the Reformation:

Who will be able to bring himself to love God with all his heart when he created hell seething with eternal torments in order to punish his own misdeeds in his victims as though he took delight in human torments?
>*De libero arbitrio* [On free will] 1524 trans. Rupp and Marlow in *The Library of Christian classics* vol. 1 Westminster Press Philadelphia 1969

Luther replied:

This is the highest degree of faith, to believe him merciful when he saves so few and damns so many, and to believe him righteous when by his own will he makes us necessarily damnable.
>*De servo arbitrio* [On the bondage of the will] 1525 trans. Watson and Drewery in *The Library of Christian classics* vol. 1

But this is not a view that Milton was prepared to take. He was so determined to refute it that he made God argue against it at considerable length.

Free will and predestination

> if I foreknew,
> Foreknowledge had no influence on their fault,
> Which had no less proved certain unforeknown.   III 117

God argues that the fall of man would have happened even if he had not foreseen it; therefore he is not responsible for it. Milton used the same argument in *De doctrina christiana*, comparing the case of a prophet who is not held to blame for what he foresees. But the prophet is not omnipotent; God *is*, and therefore can alter what he foresees (by a miracle, for instance) if it is against his will. Of course, this means he must also foresee that he is going to alter it. This circular argument leads to one of two conclusions: (1) things can happen which God does not will; therefore he is not omnipotent; (2) God has willed everything that happens, good or evil; therefore man has no free will.

Mainstream Christianity has always rejected the first of these views, though there are probably a good many people who believe that evil is as powerful as good, which comes to the same thing. The second view necessarily implies predestination: that is, God's eternal decision to save some of the human race and damn the rest, regardless of anything any of them might do in the whole course of their lives. Predestination is the ugly side of the belief in the omnipotence of God. It is one thing to say that man doesn't deserve salvation and owes it entirely to God's mercy, but quite another to say what logically follows: that it's also God alone that he has to thank for his damnation. Thus, though predestination is implied in most orthodox Christian writers from the time of St Paul, how far they chose to emphasize it was more a matter of tactics than anything else. As you can see from the Erasmus–Luther interchange, both men recognized that the doctrine was an appalling one; the difference was that Erasmus was primarily afraid that men would fall into despair whereas Luther was more afraid that they would be smug.

As for Milton, what he was most concerned about was man's responsibility, which for him necessarily meant man's freedom. God's first speech sounds harsh precisely because it insists on that freedom. It agrees with St Augustine that 'a creature which sins by its free will is more excellent than one that does not sin because it is without free will' (*The free choice of the will* 387–95, trans. Russell 1968). It might be useful to compare God's treatment of Adam and Eve with Prospero's, in *The tempest*, of Ferdinand and Miranda. The comparison is implied by Ferdinand himself when he says, 'So rare a wondered father and a wise Makes this place Paradise' (IV i). But Prospero keeps both Ariel and Caliban in bondage, and tests Ferdinand and Miranda only in a carefully controlled situation. Are freedom and happiness incompatible?

III 135–343   *The promise of redemption*

Argument. The Son of God renders praise to his Father for the manifestation of his gracious purpose towards man; but God again declares, that grace cannot be extended toward man without the satisfaction of divine justice; man hath offended the majesty of God by aspiring to Godhead; and therefore with all his progeny devoted to death must die, unless someone can be found sufficient to answer for his offence and undergo his punishment. The Son of God freely offers himself a ransom for man: the Father accepts him, ordains his incarnation, pronounces his exaltation above all names in heaven and earth; commands all the angels to adore him...

The Son

God's first speech began with the biblical phrase 'only begotten Son' (III 80). It is a difficult concept to understand, because the names of Father and Son can be used metaphorically: eg St Augustine was a Father of the church; 17th-century friends and imitators of Ben Jonson called themselves 'sons of Ben'; and the Son himself refers to man as God's 'youngest son' (III 151). In *Paradise regained* Satan repeatedly tries to find out what is meant by this title as applied to Jesus:

> The Son of God I also am, or was,
> And if I was, I am; relation stands;
> All men are Sons of God.   IV 518

The difference between the Son and other sons is summed up in the emphatic 'begotten, not created' of the Nicene Creed. God *created* the angels and the whole universe out of the raw material of Chaos; he *created* man out of earth and woman out of man; only the second person of the trinity can actually be described as being of one substance with God himself. As for the third person of the trinity, the holy spirit, we may as well forget about it since Milton seems to have done so and it is mentioned only briefly in the Bible. The concept of three-in-one probably derives from Greek thought; there are many triads in neo-platonism, for instance, because of the belief that two things required a third to bind them together, and Wind's *Pagan mysteries in the renaissance* shows many illustrations of pagan gods in a 'trinity' relationship like the one Milton contrived for Satan, Sin and Death. For the purposes of *PL*, all that matters is the Father–Son relationship.

It is not particularly hard to grasp the fact that Father and Son may be two ways of speaking about the same thing: on the one hand, the embodiment of all goodness, power and truth; on the other, these attributes put into action. The difficulty really comes when one part of the trinity acts independently, as in the sacrifice of Christ, whose prayer in the garden of Gethsemane was 'not my will but thine be done' (*Luke* xxii 42). That the Son should be one with the Father and yet distinct from him was a mystical paradox, and it's not surprising that many theologians tried to get rid of one or the other half of this doctrine in the interest of a more 'logical' approach. At one extreme is the view that God himself actually died on the cross; at the other, a refusal to see Father and Son as co-eternal or equal. Milton was himself logical rather than

20

mystical, and in *De doctrina christiana* he emphasized the humanity of Christ as also the subordination of the Son to the Father: 'Undoubtedly the product of reason must be something consistent with reason, not a notion as absurd as it is removed from all human comprehension', such as the notion that Christ's relation to man was simultaneously that of judge and counsel for the defence.

But he didn't go so far as to become heretical, like the Arians who maintained that the Son was created rather than begotten and raised to divinity only by God's command:

Milton differentiates between the Father and the Son *only* during their verbal exchanges in the various councils that took place in Heaven, but as soon as these councils end and the Godhead acts beyond the confines of Heaven the distinction between the two persons is abruptly dropped. Thus during the council before the creation of the universe the Father and the Son are clearly differentiated (VII. 131 ff.), but once the Creator embarks on his mission outside Heaven he is specifically termed 'God'. During the council after the Fall of Man the Father and the Son are again clearly differentiated (X. 21 ff.), but once the Judge leaves Heaven for the Garden of Eden he is once again termed 'God', even 'the Lord God' (X. 163).

C. A. PATRIDES *M and the Christian tradition* Clarendon Press 1966

There is a rabbinical tradition that God, in the beginning, created a world based on justice alone. This didn't work, so he destroyed it and created another based on mercy alone, but it was a failure too. Finally he replaced it with the world as we know it, based on the union of justice with mercy. This legend might almost be a parable of the Father's relation to the Son. You may like to trace this relation in the style of their speeches. Notice that the Son, like the Father, makes puns:

> O Father, gracious was that word which closed
> Thy sovereign sentence, that man should find grace   III 144

where *word* and *sentence* both have double meanings and *grace* and *gracious* echo each other. There is a similar echo effect in other repetitions, insistent, pleading. Compare the terse, fast-moving logic of the Father's lines:

> The first sort by their own suggestion fell,
> Self-tempted, self-depraved: man falls deceived
> By the other first: man therefore shall find grace,
> The other none   III 129

which could easily be read as prose. There is a striking contrast, too, between the precision of the Father's language and the vague, lyrical tone of the passage bridging his speech and the Son's. His words fill heaven with 'ambrosial fragrance' and 'joy ineffable' and the lines introducing the Son might even be read as a detached rhyming quatrain:

> Most glorious, in him all his Father shone
> Substantially expressed, and in his face
> Divine compassion visibly appeared,
> Love without end, and without measure grace.   III 139

Grace

Grace in movement or manners means something unforced, natural, not worked at. The same is true of grace in the theological sense. As the Son says, it 'Comes unprevented [ie unanticipated], unimplored, unsought' (III 231). Those who received the grace of God were the *elect*, the chosen few who were to be saved. According to Calvin, these were also the only ones to be offered it in the first place. Milton, however, believed that the choice was man's, and God declares that he will harden only those hearts which are already hard:

> This my long sufferance and my day of grace
> They who neglect and scorn, shall never taste;
> But hard be hardened, blind be blinded more.   III 198

Even God's promise of 'peculiar grace' to some 'elect above the rest', although frankly arbitrary ('so is my will'), refers only to special spiritual gifts. The rest of mankind will also be given a chance, and some will profit by it. But 'no one believes because God has foreseen his belief, but God foresees his belief because he was about to believe' (*De doctrina christiana* 'Of predestination').

The way in which God says he will offer grace to men is by a series of metaphorical lights: conscience (the light of nature), divine revelation (the light of grace) and eventually the vision of the heavenly kingdom (the light of glory):

> Light after light well used they shall attain,
> And to the end persisting, safe arrive.   III 196

This notion of a progression from nature to grace to glory was particularly important to the reformers because it held out the hope that eventually justice would not only be done (as the doctrine of predestination implied) but also be seen to be done.

By the light of nature it is an insoluble problem how it can be just that a good man should suffer and a bad man prosper; but this problem is solved by the light of grace. By the light of grace it is an insoluble problem how God can damn one who is unable by any power of his own to do anything but sin and be guilty... But the light of glory tells us differently, and it will show us hereafter that the God whose judgement here is one of incomprehensible righteousness is a God of most perfect and manifest righteousness. In the meantime, we can only *believe* this...

LUTHER De servo arbitrio

Redemption

The word means 'buying back', and hence the subject of Christ's sacrifice tends to be treated in legalistic language; see Herbert's *Redemption*. In particular, writers from the time of St Paul onward played a series of variations on one theme: Christ equals Adam raised to the nth power.

For since by man came death, by man came also the resurrection of the dead. For as in Adam all die, even so in Christ shall all be made alive.

I Corinthians xv

Both God and the Son similarly insist on the parallel:

> Which of ye will be mortal to redeem
> Man's mortal crime, and just the unjust to save   III 214
>
> Behold me then, me for him, life for life
> I offer   III 236
>
>   So man, as is most just,
> Shall satisfy for man, be judged and die,
> And dying rise, and rising with him raise
> His brethren, ransomed with his own dear life.   III 294

The pendulum swing effect produced by these repetitions finally culminates in triumph – 'So heavenly love shall outdo hellish hate' (III 298) – and looks forward to Adam's reaction at the end of the poem when the pattern has been explained to him:

> O goodness infinite, goodness immense!
> That all this good of evil shall produce,
> And evil turn to good; more wonderful
> Than that which by creation first brought forth
> Light out of darkness! Full of doubt I stand,
> Whether I should repent me now of sin
> By me done and occasioned, or rejoice
> Much more, that much more good thereof shall spring,
> To God more glory, more good will to men
> From God, and over wrath grace shall abound.   XII 469

Nevertheless there is silence in heaven when God first asks for a volunteer to make all this possible by dying in place of the human race. What Milton may have had in mind at this point is a passage from *Revelation* v:

Then I saw in the right hand of the One who sat on the throne a scroll, with writing inside and out, and it was sealed up with seven seals. And I saw a mighty angel proclaiming in a loud voice, 'Who is worthy to open the scroll and to break its seals?' There was no one in heaven or on earth or under the earth able to open the scroll or to look inside it. I was in tears because no one was found who was worthy to open the scroll or to look inside it. But one of the elders said to me: 'Do not weep; for the Lion from the tribe of Judah, the Scion of David, has won the right to open the scroll and break its seven seals.'

Then I saw standing in the very middle of the throne, inside the circle of living creatures and the circle of elders, a Lamb with the marks of slaughter upon him.

Later, 'when the Lamb broke the seventh seal, there was silence in heaven for what seemed half an hour' (viii). Milton rarely uses such visionary language as this (notice the dreamlike substitution of the sacrificed Lamb for the conquering Lion described by the angel); he sticks to 'forfeiture' and 'ransom'; but the Lion–Lamb antithesis is basic to the whole poem. The suspense at this point obviously parallels the similar silence at II 418–26 before Satan offers to go on *his* mission to earth, and must be meant (whichever passage was written first) as another example of heavenly love out-doing hellish hate. But all these parallels can work both ways. *Why* do all the angels stand silent? Can they understand what is being asked of them? Could they be mortal, even if they wanted to? 'Where shall we find such love?' God asks; the angels are virtually embodiments of the love of God (the highest order, the seraphim, were traditionally thought of as made of fire because they *burned* in their love), but this means only that they love to the full extent of their capacity for loving, which is not infinite. If they don't even speak on man's behalf, much less offer to die for him, it may be that their sense of justice is stronger than their love. One can see why God says that the victim must be 'able, and as willing' (III 211).

But the Son is silent too. His hesitation, which makes him seem 'human' even before his incarnation, ought to draw our attention to the full horror of what he agrees to in saying 'on me let thine anger fall'. Milton must surely be thinking not only of the cry from the cross – 'My God, my God, why hast thou forsaken me?' (*Mark* xv 34) – but also of the puritan commentators' insistence that at that moment God had not only withdrawn his love from his Son but was unleashing on him 'such a sea of his wrath as was equivalent to the sins of the whole world' (William Perkins *A golden chain, or the description of theology* 1592). Since God's proposal makes no provision for a resurrection, it must sound to all those present as if they are being asked to volunteer to separate themselves eternally from the love which motivates their entire existence, in order to rescue human beings who justly deserve to die anyway.

The Son recognizes that if God has decreed that 'man shall find grace' he must also have decreed the means by which this shall happen. The rest is faith.

The Son cannot know any more than others at the council that the task named does not mean annihilation. The moment of silence includes his silence to underscore the clear enormity of the solution. When after that moment's hesitation he offers to die for man, he does not know that the death he undertakes will not be final; he *trusts* that the omnipotence whose goodness he does know will not permit injustice... Freely the Son makes his choice of word and deed; and if the choice has been foreknown, foreknowledge had no influence on his virtue.

IRENE SAMUEL from 'The dialogue in Heaven: a reconsideration of *PL* III 1–417' *Publications of the Modern Language Association* LXXII 1957

III 344–415 *Heaven*

Argument. ...they obey, and hymning to their harps in full choir, celebrate the Father and the Son.

This, like the end of God's preceding speech about the end of the world, is based on *Revelation* v. When the Lamb takes the book with the seven seals, he is celebrated by songs from the full host of heaven:

Then as I looked I heard the voices of countless angels. These were all round the throne and the living creatures and the elders. Myriads upon myriads there were, thousands upon thousands, and they cried aloud:
'Worthy is the Lamb, the Lamb that was slain, to receive all power and wealth, wisdom and might, honour and glory and praise!'

In Milton's early plans for a drama on the fall of man, such songs would have supplied the place of the Greek tragedy chorus:

The Apocalypse of St John is the majestic image of a high and stately tragedy, shutting up and intermingling her solemn scenes and acts with a sevenfold chorus of hallelujahs and harping symphonies.

The reason of church government urged against prelaty 1642

Most of the details of Milton's heaven come from this book: the angels casting their crowns before the throne, the sea of glass, the golden harps, the bowls of incense representing human prayers (see *PL* XI 14–25). Much of the biblical imagery evokes precious stones:

On the throne sat one whose appearance was like the gleam of jasper and cornelian; and round the throne there was a rainbow, bright as an emerald. *Revelation* ix

In one way this is appropriate – precious stones are not only beautiful, their value depends on what one is prepared to give for them – but in another it's offensive, because (1) it's materialistic and (2) heaven *shouldn't* be compared to anything else. Similes fall flat in face of absolute reality.

I think Milton knew this. He had already given Mammon a description of just such a scene as is evoked here:

> with what eyes could we
> Stand in his presence humble, and receive
> Strict laws imposed, to celebrate his throne
> With warbled hymns, and to his Godhead sing
> Forced hallelujahs; while he lordly sits
> Our envied sovereign, and his altar breathes
> Ambrosial odours and ambrosial flowers,
> Our servile offerings? This must be our task
> In heaven, this our delight; how wearisome
> Eternity so spent in worship paid
> To whom we hate. II 239

Mammon is quite right; worship without love is only empty ceremony. The answer to his speech comes later from Raphael:

> freely we serve,
> Because we freely love, as in our will
> To love or not. V 538

Heaven, like hell, is a state of mind.

In the descriptive passage which acts as a 'preamble sweet' to the angels' song, the sheer difficulty of the syntax may show Milton's embarrassment at having to combine metaphorical and literal concepts of heaven, but it may also be a way of creating a timeless atmosphere (note use of present tense, and the peculiar tense sequence throughout) as well as keeping the picture from becoming too concrete. Is the pavement made of jasper, or just *like* jasper? Is the amaranth plant growing on earth or in heaven? Is the 'fount of life' separate from God or a metaphor for him? Is 'heaven' the subject or the object of 'rung'? As if to show that all comparisons are pointless, Milton even introduces a curious non-simile –

> a shout
> Loud as from numbers without number, sweet
> As from blest voices, uttering joy...   III 345

– which means simply that the shout sounds like innumerable voices, which it is, and blest voices, which they are.

Is Milton quoting or describing when he writes 'Thee Father first they sung' (III 372)? Who is speaking – Milton or the angels – in the last lines of the song?

> Hail, Son of God, saviour of men, thy name
> Shall be the copious matter of my song
> Henceforth, and never shall my harp thy praise
> Forget, nor from thy Father's praise disjoin.   III 412

As Broadbent points out (*Some graver subject* 1960), this 'brings the episode in a circle from "Hail holy light" to "Hail Son of God, Saviour of Men"'. It also shows how much more exciting the concept of God looks from the outside than from the inside.

III 416–97   *The paradise of fools*

Argument. Mean while Satan alights upon the bare convex of this world's outermost orb; where wandering he first finds a place since called the Limbo of Vanity; what persons and things fly up thither.

The alternation of close-up and long-shot continues as Milton moves away from identification with the angels' song to focus on Satan again and on the difference between the pretty jewel-like universe which he saw in the distance at the end of Book II and the unfriendly place he actually finds:

> a globe far off
> It seemed, now seems a boundless continent
> Dark, waste, and wild...   III 422

Later arrivals at this place are going to be disappointed too. Notice how Milton prepares the tone of the fools' paradise passage by the way he describes Satan: a vulture, a Tartar (by implication), a 'fiend'. Is this why he keeps reminding us (three times) that Satan is *walking* instead of flying? Or is this a foreshadowing of his later career?

And the Lord said unto Satan, 'Whence comest thou?' Then Satan answered the Lord, and said, 'From going to and fro in the earth, and from walking up and down in it.'   *Job* i

The elaborate vulture simile works on several levels:

Satan = vulture   preying on   lambs and kids = mankind
                               (cf parable of sheep and goats)
     and Tartar   invading   India = paradise (which some
                               believed to have been sited
                               here).

But the curious geographical lore about the Chinese sail-wagons at another 'windy sea of land' in a convenient halfway location seems to me grotesque – Milton's way of warning us that we are moving from epic into satire. In *Lycidas*, St Peter's attack on the corrupt clergy is similarly set off from the rest of the poem; its style is similar too – 'blind mouths', 'lean and flashy songs', 'swoll'n with wind'.

What adds to the distinctive tone of the limbo passage is that it's the most obvious borrowing in *PL*. In Ariosto's *Orlando furioso* a similar limbo is located on the moon (a natural enough idea, considering the etymology of 'lunatic'), and Milton goes out of his way to say that Ariosto got it wrong; human folly and vanity don't belong

> in the neighbouring moon, as some have dreamed;
> Those argent fields more likely habitants,
> Translated saints, or middle spirits hold
> Betwixt the angelical and human kind.   III 459

This, of course, is logical too, since the moon was supposed to be a meeting-point of the mortal and immortal parts of the universe; the Attendant Spirit in *Comus* comes from there. Logical or not, however, Milton didn't really believe, any more than Ariosto, that the afterlife could be described in geographical terms. Limbo and purgatory were both fictitious for him, and the passage is pure fantasy.

Milton was extremely fond of this part of the *Orlando furioso*; he even translated a couple of lines from it in one of his political pamphlets. It seems to have been present in his mind throughout Book III. Ariosto's hero Astolfo – an *English* knight – rides a winged horse, restores the sight of a blind king, and visits not only the moon but also hell and Eden, the earthly paradise. In Eden he meets St John, author of *Revelation*, who lives there with two other 'translated saints', Enoch and Elijah. St John takes him to the moon in a fiery chariot and, like Milton's muse, tempers the air through which they travel so that they won't be scorched by the sphere of fire. The vanities which Astolfo sees on the moon include those of religion:

> Of mingled broth he saw a mighty mass
>> That to no use all spilt on ground did lie,
>> He asked his teacher, and he heard it was
>> The fruitless alms that men give when they die.

But most of his targets (except alchemy) are different from Milton's:

> Some lose their wit with love, some with ambition,
>> Some running to the sea, great wealth to get,
>> Some following lords, and men of high condition,
>> And some in fair jewels rich and costly set:
>> One hath desire to prove a rare magician,
>> And some with poetry their wit forget,
>> Another thinks to be an alchemist,
>> Till all be spent, and he his number missed.
>>> trans. Harington 1591

The crude language is also Milton's own, with the implications of 'wind' and 'backside' taken as far as possible, in the manner of his earlier satires on the bishops:

O what a death it is to the prelates to be thus unvisarded, thus uncased, to have the periwigs plucked off that cover your baldness, your inside nakedness thrown open to public view!
Animadversions upon the remonstrant's defence against
Smectymnuus 1641

But the satire also points at both Satan (bound on a 'transitory and vain' errand) and, potentially, at Milton himself. The desire for fame, which is one of the vanities he punishes with limbo, is described in *Lycidas* as 'That last infirmity of noble mind'.

III 498–590   *Satan enters the universe*

Argument. ...thence comes to the gate of heaven, described ascending by stairs, and the waters above the firmament that flow about it: his passage thence to the orb of the sun...

Jacob's ladder

The simple ladder of the original vision becomes, in Milton, a characteristic baroque staircase leading up to a jewel-encrusted gate. Are we supposed to take it literally? It seems to be solid enough for Satan to stand on the bottom step, and the reason why it's drawn halfway up instead of extending all the way to earth is presumably that otherwise the rest of his journey would be too easy. On the other hand, each step is said to have a symbolic meaning and it is difficult to see what practical purpose the structure serves: the angels normally fly to earth or (like Uriel in IV 555–6) ride on a sunbeam, while new arrivals in heaven are said to cross the jasper sea by air or water transport (III 518–22).

Jacob's vision at Bethel was described in *Genesis* xxviii:

And he dreamed, and, behold, a ladder set up on the earth, and the top of it reached to heaven: and, behold, the angels of God ascending and descending on it. And, behold, the Lord stood above it, and said, I am the Lord God of Abraham thy father, and the God of Isaac: the land whereon thou liest, to thee will I give it, and to thy seed...And Jacob awaked out of his sleep, and he said, Surely the Lord is in this place, and I knew it not. And he was afraid, and said, How dreadful is this place! this is none other but the house of God, and this is the gate of heaven.

It was at Bethel that Jacob later wrestled with an angel and, considering it holy ground, he built an altar there to God. Yet the Bible also records that an altar with a golden calf was set up in the same spot – and shattered by divine power – many generations later (see *I Kings* xii 28–xiii 5). So it's appropriate that Satan should appear at this most sacred of places. Is this perhaps a continuation of Milton's satire on pilgrimages and the belief that one place was inherently any holier than another? Notice all the 'up' and 'down' references throughout the passage. A ladder can lead in either direction; Satan is on the lowest step of the ascent to heaven but instead he looks – and eventually moves – downward. It is the physical acting out of the choice which he makes more explicitly in his next soliloquy (IV 79–113).

Milton's astronomy

We are given two pictures of the universe in III, seen from two different directions.

1. *Fool's-eye-view*. As the various dupes head for the paradise of fools,

> They pass the planets seven, and pass the fixed,
> And that crystalline sphere whose balance weighs
> The trepidation talked, and that first moved...   III 481

The 'planets seven' include the sun and moon; the 'fixed' is the sphere in which all the stars were thought to be embedded as in clear jelly. The heavenly bodies were not seen as moving of their own accord in empty space; rather, they were thought to be attached to their own transparent strips of sky – the spheres – which touched and interlocked in such a way that they could all be moved at once from the outside by the rapid whirling of the *primum mobile* (some writers actually thought 'world' came from *whirled*). At the same time, they also had motions of their own, in the opposite direction to that of the *primum mobile*; this was supposed to explain differences in their speed and in their paths through the sky.

All this is extremely old-fashioned for 1667. Since Milton shows himself considerably more open-minded on the subject elsewhere in the poem, I suspect that he is deliberately sticking to a traditional cosmology to go with the equally traditional theme of the journey through the spheres (see Donne's *Second anniversary* 1612, 185–206, for another example). It is only in this fantasy context that he refers to the crystalline sphere, whose existence was less universally accepted than the other landmarks of this description.

The crystalline sphere was invented as a result of certain misapprehensions concerning the precession of the equinoxes. Precession is the small annual westward shift of the sun in relation to the stars. A given constellation rises a little later each year on a given date; and thus, through the centuries, the stars seem to wheel slowly eastward. The sidereal revolution is completed in about 25,800 years. Some Greek theorists believed that the stars' change of position in relation to the sun was an oscillation, an alternating forward and backward motion of the stellar sphere with a slowing down before and a speeding up after each reversal. After some centuries, precession would become recession. The Arabians, adopting and elaborating this theory, introduced the crystalline sphere. The poles of the stellar (the eighth) sphere, they supposed, were joined to the inner surface of the crystalline sphere, each pole very slowly describing a small circle on this surface, thus accounting for the supposed reversals of direction and the variation of speed. A slow eastward drift of the ninth sphere explained completion of the cycle.

LAWRENCE BABB *The moral cosmos of PL*
Michigan State U.P. 1970

The jasper sea, which surrounds heaven like a moat, and which Milton identifies in his *Argument* with the biblical 'waters above the firmament', comes from an even older cosmology than Aristotle's. The Hebrews also believed in a multi-layered universe resting on pillars. Milton refers briefly to this theory in *Comus* 597 but in *PL* he has very little to say about it.

2. *Satan's-eye-view.* As soon as Satan launches himself into the universe, we get a very different impression, full of the excitement of seventeenth-century astronomical discussion: perhaps the stars are inhabited; perhaps the sun rules the planets by magnetic force; there are stunning effects of perspective as Satan first looks at, then moves among, the whole marvellous creation. He himself, despite the sneaking connotations of 'scout' and the reference to his envy, is seen again as the adventurer of II 1041–4 (and cf IV 159–65), capable of being overwhelmed by beauty; the last time that happens is just before he approaches Eve (IX 463–6).

To visualize things from Satan's position, it helps to remember that he is always on the wrong side, literally as well as morally. He lands on the hollow shell of the universe at its dark side; thus heaven is invisible to him, though he, of course, is visible to God's all-seeing eye. This hard shell, incidentally, can't be the *primum mobile*, which would have been spinning too fast for even Satan to walk on; it's a dramatic convenience rather than a serious contribution to cosmological speculation. When Satan has finally walked halfway along the circumference of this globe and looked down through the opening, he finds himself again blocked from the light, this time by the earth and its shadow which come between him and the sun. It's a box-within-a-box situation. Even when he reaches the sun itself, he approaches Uriel from behind.

What he sees from the bottom stair of heaven is basically a celestial globe on its side. As the whole universe is rotating on its poles, to left and right of Satan's downward gaze, the constellations of the zodiac are describing a circle directly beneath him, perpendicular to the polar axis and exactly parallel with the equator. This symmetry is a purely temporary state of affairs; see X 651–91 for what happened after the fall.

Alongside this imaginative expansiveness goes a surprising lyrical delicacy of tone: the almost unimaginable vastness of the universe is compared to a towered city lit by the rising sun; the constellation of Aries the ram is a 'fleecy star' (!), and Satan winds his way through the 'marble air' like a figure-skater on ice. There is a hint that the stars which he passes might be idyllic paradises like Eden; a great contemporary question, raised by Galileo's observation that the moon had mountains and valleys like the earth, was not only whether the rest of the universe was inhabited but also whether it had been affected by the fall and resurrection.

All kinds of change were associated with evil and Satan, but until Galileo announced that the moon was rugged rather than smooth and that the sun sometimes displayed dark patches it was assumed that this changeableness was confined to earth. What was perfect didn't change – couldn't change, unless for the worse. Galileo ridiculed the peripatetics – believers in the universe as described by Aristotle – for the elaborate theories they devised in order to preserve the concept of a static world:

Well, if alteration were annihilation, the Peripatetics would have some reason for concern; but since it is nothing but mutation, there is no reason for such bitter hostility to it. It seems to me unreasonable to call 'corruption in an egg that which produces a chicken'...Our special hatred of death need not render fragility odious. Why should we want to become less mutable?   *3rd letter on sunspots* 1612 (pub. 1613)

Theories which had been offered to explain away the spots on the sun were (1) that they were simply a delusion on the part of the observer or a flaw in the lens of his telescope, (2) that they were not on the surface of the sun but in the air at some distance from it – either stars orbiting it or the planet Mercury. Symbolically, these explanations have satanic repercussions: illusion, error, the deceitful god Mercury. 'Stars', in Hebrew writing, often mean angels; eg the dragon whose tail drew down a third of the stars of heaven (*Revelation* xii 4) is the traditional source for the proportion of angels who rebelled. Galileo's distinction between stars and sunspots was not intended symbolically, but it could be read that way:

Essentially they [the sunspots] have properties that differ not a little from the true stars, which are always of one shape and quite regular, while the spots are of various shapes and most irregular; the former are consistent in size and shape, the latter always instable and changing; the former are ever the same, and permanent in a manner that transcends the memories of all past ages, while the latter are capable of being produced and dissolved from one day to the next. Stars are never seen except luminous; spots are always dark, etc...

The comparison between Satan and a sunspot is, then, more complex than at first appears.

Argument. . . . he finds there Uriel the regent of that orb, but first changes himself into the shape of a meaner angel; and pretending a zealous desire to behold the new creation and man whom God had placed here, inquires of him the place of his habitation, and is directed; alights first on Mount Niphates.

The sun and alchemy

Satan is attracted to the sun as 'likest heaven' (572). Compare the dance of the planets about the sun and that of the angels about the throne of God (v 621–7), also the alchemical power of light in heaven, as described by Satan:

> Which of us who beholds the bright surface
> Of this ethereous mould whereon we stand,
> This continent of spacious heaven, adorned
> With plant, fruit, flower ambrosial, gems and gold,
> Whose eye so superficially surveys
> These things, as not to mind from whence they grow
> Deep under ground, materials dark and crude,
> Or spiritous and fiery spume, till touched
> With heaven's ray, and tempered they shoot forth
> So beauteous, opening to the ambient light.   VI 472

It's just the reverse of hell, which is hideous on the surface and has its gold and jewels beneath (1 688–709). The natural alchemy of the sun and the heavenly light is also contrasted with the unnatural sexual implications of mining in hell: 'Rifled the bowels of their mother earth'. . .'Opened. . .a spacious wound'. . . 'digged out ribs of gold'. The alchemists similarly tried to speed up a natural process (coition between sun and earth) by the use of fire and male and female elements (mercury and sulphur). A further parallel with Satan's activities, especially at this point in the book, was their fraud and hypocrisy. The finder of the philosopher's stone was supposed to be a holy man yet his main motive was greed. Jonson's *Alchemist* 1610 shows up this parody of religious symbolism:

> *Surly.*   I'll believe
> That Alchemy is a pretty kind of game,
> Somewhat like tricks o' the cards, to cheat a man
> With charming.
> *Subtle.*   Sir?

Surly.   What else are all your terms,
Whereon no one of your writers 'grees with other?
Of your elixir, your *lac virginis*,
Your stone, your med'cine and your chrysosperme,
Your sal, your sulphur, and your mercury,
Your oil of height, your tree of life, your blood,
Your marchesite, your tutie, your magnesia,
Your toad, your crow, your dragon, and your panther,
Your sun, your moon, your firmament, your adrop,
Your lato, azoch, zernich, chilbrit, heautarit,
And then your red man, and your white woman,
With all your broths, your menstrues, and materials,
Of piss and egg-shells, women's terms, man's blood,
Hair o' the head, burnt clouts, chalk, merds, and clay,
Powder of bones, scalings of iron, glass,
And worlds of other strange ingredients,
Would burst a man to name?...
Subtle. Was not all the knowledge
Of the Egyptians writ in mystic symbols?
Speak not the Scriptures oft in parables?   II iii

Uriel

All Milton's angels except Michael, Raphael and Gabriel have
names drawn either from the Apocrypha or from the long tradition
of Judeo-Christian mysticism, which was full of speculation about
the names and natures of the angels. Protestants, with their distrust
of all tradition not based on scripture, generally took the view of
William Perkins (*The golden chain* 1592): 'That there are degrees
of angels it is most plain, but it is not for us to search who or how
many there be of each order; neither ought we curiously to in-
quire how they are distinguished, whether in essence, gifts or
offices.' Milton essentially follows this advice; his use of names
seems arbitrary and he seldom bothers to discriminate in his
references to the various ranks: thrones, dominations, archangels,
cherubim, seraphim, etc.

Uriel's name comes from the apocryphal *Book of Esdras*, where
he answers the prophet's Job-like questions about God's ways to
men, but the scriptural authority for an angel on the sun (*Revela-
tion* xix) is really used to justify a bit of platonism. Plato thought
that the stars and planets were visible gods whose motions were
guided by intelligences; Christian writers identified these in-
telligences with the angels, drawing also on the biblical symbols of
stars, lamps, eyes, etc. Even Uriel's account of creation is more
platonic than biblical (except in its stress on the *word*). It's based
on the idea that form and matter are separate (Plato's own example

35

is a gold triangle: the matter is gold and the form is a triangle) and that the process of bringing order out of disorder (chaos) was one of imparting a soul (form) to matter. Compare also Plato's account of how the creator gave life to the stars:

The divine form he made mostly of fire so that it should be as bright and beautiful to look at as possible; and he made it spherical like the universe and set it to follow the movement of the highest intelligence, distributing it round the circle of the heaven to be a kind of universal cosmic embroidery...This is the origin of the fixed stars, which are living beings divine and eternal and remain always rotating in the same place and in the same sense.   *Timaeus* trans. H. D. P. Lee, Penguin 1965

Satan's deception of Uriel is used, rather like Iago's deceptions of Roderigo and Cassio, to prepare us for the success of another deception later on. Evil rarely has even the smallest triumph over goodness in Milton: 'wicked, and thence weak' (IV 856) is his more usual view. But compare

> goodness thinks no ill
> Where no ill seems   III 688

and Edmund's account of Edgar in *Lear*:

> a brother noble,
> Whose nature is so far from doing harms
> That he suspects none; on whose foolish honesty
> My practices ride easy.   I ii

What is our attitude to the holy fool of eg Dostoyevsky, the born loser doomed by his very goodness? Are we pessimistic about good in an evil world? or just contemptuous?

It is not because angels are holier than men or devils that makes them angels, but because they do not expect holiness from one another, but from God only.   BLAKE *A vision of the last judgment* 1810

Introduction to Book IV

Contents of the Book

Milton's special contributions to the myth

A ranging command of all the various references to paradise in geography and poetry...manifest in some of the similes eg Hesperian fables, Mount Amara...other similes are more down-to-earth eg the ploughman and here is another contribution: the solid smells and tangibility of Milton's paradise...hence the dignity of Adam and Eve, statuesque yet distinctly naked.

From the nakedness, and the affirmations of marriage, come the attacks on hypocrites, ie on Roman catholics and other political enemies of his own day (cf Satan at 193 like one of the hireling priests of *Lycidas*)...hence the whole political struggle of the 17th century.

That local struggle is paralleled also by the cosmic struggle elements – Uriel, Gabriel, Ithuriel and Zephon, the military activity, the flytings between Satan and good angels while Adam and Eve sleep. Yet the cosmic struggle inverts the 17th-century one: Satan is the rebellious parallel to Milton...hence the insults are inconclusive, and the accusations of being a cringing courtier are mutual (945–59).

So we have a solidly established marriage, related extraneously to political issues in history and in eternity: my white, and your black, are infinitely right and wrong. The marriage is also related to the cosmos by its moral rhetoric (eg 'upright...mysterious'); and by the lyrics of Adam and Eve: they tie their love into the universe ('All seasons and their change') and into the creator ('Maker omnipotent')...Hence the sexual politics of the book.

Sexual politics are perhaps the centre of these Miltonic specialities, tying all together: 'God is thy law, thou mine' says Eve to Adam (637). Vertically,

> God
> Adam
> Eve

The pattern breaks the pairing Adam + Eve; it puts her onto the lowest rational rung; hence easiest for Satan to assail. He does, with the dream – the imagination's version of chaos, rebellion, denial of order:

		God			
		worship	worship		
male	Adam			Gabriel	good angel
	love			hate	
female	Eve		dream	Satan	bad angel

But it is a denial which is sexual (so a part of Adam) and poetic (so a part of Milton).

What paradise implies about fallen life

Under its leaf he watched through peacocktwittering lashes the southing sun. I am caught in this burning scene. Pan's hour, the faunal noon. Among gumheavy serpentplants, milkoozing fruits, where on the tawny waters leaves lie wide. Pain is far.   JAMES JOYCE *Ulysses* 1922

To ask where I come from is to ask who I am. There are many answers; the *kind* of answer is itself an answer. If I say 'I have evolved from *homo erectus*, the animal with the highest intelligence and the most complex organization of the Middle Pleistocene', I do not contradict the statement 'I come from Adam and Eve': but I present myself in a different perspective; I apply another mode of consciousness of self. I also imply two different sorts of change that have occurred: between *homo erectus* and me, or between Adam and Eve and me (Adam = Hebrew man = Latin *homo*; Eve = Hebrew life). One is described in terms of biology, the other in terms of ethics. They overlap.

Here are some of the changes implied by Milton's answers:

	origin	*change*	*present*
A1	image of God	degradation	'To such unsightly sufferings debased' XI 510
2	divine	loss of divinity	human
3	fully human	loss of humanity	subhuman
4	*homo erectus*	evolution	*homo sapiens*
5	primitive		civilized
6	childlike		adult
B1	innocence	fall	guilt by original sin
2	not conscious of self		conscious of self, and of that consciousness
C	nakedness		clothed
D1	sexual dimorphism		
2	androgyne		
E	parents, ancestors		children, descendants
F1	Eve made of Adam's rib		
2	The Great Mother		
G	dream		reality
H	communism		private property
I	'sweet gardening labour'		work
J	the garden of God		Spaceship Earth
K	'the sun's more potent ray...old Ocean smiled'		

You can fill in blanks, and lengthen the list. Note especially that you can start from the other end and get a different answer: eg under A6 if you see the originals as childlike (as the theologian Irenaeus did) you must see yourself as adult, or sophisticated; but if you see yourself as a child you must see them as parents.

The sections that follow take up some of these states and changes. Because they are to do with human nature, they require communal work; if you are alone, you may need to take several parts to achieve the full picture.

A. *The image of God*

In their looks divine the image of their glorious maker shone   291

Imagine in writing the first recognizably human creatures: two of them perform a specific simple action. Against that, imagine the process when a child 'recognizes' a parent in the distance; and write of a grandparent who sees a grown-up child sitting beside its parents.

Some early commentators on *Genesis* thought Adam and Eve were divine (A2) so what they lost by their fall was something extra to the human; others, including Milton (for this was the protestant doctrine), thought Adam and Eve were perfectly human (3) so what they lost and we haven't got is full humanity. There was argument about whether, having lost the 'image' of God, we may still have the 'similitude' – still look like him: see XI 510. For Milton the worst loss had political force: it was of reason, and liberty (XIII 83). What would unfallen politics be like? Consider how a person looks when you are in love with him; and afterwards.

B. *Innocence*

Not to taste that only tree of knowledge   423

Establish our different usages for the word *innocent*. (Of course all our usages are by definition tainted with original sin.) The 17th-century poet Vaughan has an un-Miltonic view – the 'white celestial thought' of childhood (*The retreat*). A child is perhaps not innocent, even in a court of law, in the same sense as an adult? For the myth generally, the tree, and the nature of sin, work from *PL: introduction* pp. 11–25 and *PL* IX–X ed. J.M. Evans pp. 160–75 in this series. In the chart above, original sin means sin inherited from our origins, like genes. You may have experience of more specific inheritance.

C. *Nakedness*

So passed they naked on, nor shunned the sight of God or angel 319

A highly specific manifestation of innocence. Milton remarks on it several times here, and at V 383; sexual shame is an early sign of sin after the fall:

> innocence, that as a veil
> Had shadowed them from knowing ill, was gone,
> Just confidence, and native righteounsess,
> And honour from about them, naked left
> To guilty shame... IX 1054

For Milton, shame is distinctly not inherent in the body; it is a product of sin, of knowing and thinking 'ill'. Historically speaking this is uniquely free, and brave. There are affirmations of the body in love poetry, notably Donne's *Elegy XIX To his mistress going to bed:*

> Full nakedness, all joys are due to thee.
> As souls unbodied, bodies unclothed must be
> To taste whole joys...
> Then since I may know,
> As liberally as to a midwife show
> Thyself: cast all, yea, this white linen hence,
> Here is no penance, much less innocence.
> To teach thee, I am naked first: why then
> What needst thou have more covering than a man?

But you might define the fallen, in its weakness and its glories, by the characteristics of that verse. See Robert Hodge's appendix to *PL* VI in this series, pp. 155–7. Painting was richer and freer, not confining the naked to the erotic; yet even there the best work is perhaps that which most fully accepts and explores the loss of God's image: Rembrandt's paintings of his ageing wife with wrinkled thighs.

But Milton's own attitude is fraught with anxiety (naturally enough). He projects it angrily onto hypocrites (744), those to whom all things are impure, concerned with 'mere shows of seeming pure' (316). It is just, partial, and political: for he sets up a series of what is for him the genuinely pure: no clothes for Adam and Eve = no vestments for priests; purity of sex in Eden = no vice at court (767) and no need for consecrated churches or marriage services (736 ff); Adam's nakedness when he goes to meet Raphael at V 351 is 'More solemn than the tedious pomp that waits On princes'. To use Milton we have to admit in what ways

we – the people in our immediate group – are primitivistic –
clothes? music? – and how much of this behaviour approaches a
genuine free puritanism, how much is weaponry, a means of
projecting rage at social and political enemies? You may find it
easier to do this for other people than for yourself.

D. Sexual dimorphism
Manlike, but different sex   VIII 471

You might look at the men and women with you and write what it
is that tells you the difference. It is what *they* write that may be
illuminating. Or you could try painting Adam and Eve at this
stage, as you think a person would see them who is of different sex
from you. In the *Symposium*, Plato tells the myth of an andro-
gynous original being; the fall consisted in its splitting into two,
male and female (each then goes about looking for its other half).
Some people see sexual dimorphism as a tyranny of the genital,
and hope we shall evolve into something more like Plato's andro-
gyne. So the myths go in opposite directions, 1–2 and 2–1.

   Giedion (quoted on the image of God in appendix) points to the
survival into civilized Babylonian and Egyptian art of certain
prehistoric perceptions of the female: narrow thorax, huge but-
tocks, and sharply defined pelvic triangle enclosing the vulva.
The steatopygiac buttock still characterizes Bushmen, who were
far more numerous than European tribes until quite recently; it
has to do with fat reserves, and development of striding muscles.
Milton would seem to be, and all European painters certainly are,
inaccurately racist in their depiction of early man. You might
attempt to describe a parent as if black or, if you are black, as if
white, and so on.

E. Parents
From us two a race to fill the earth   732

Chart the allusions – they're mostly implied – to children, and
what their context is.

F. Eve made of Adam's rib
Though both not equal, as their sex not equal seemed   295

They are not constantly parents: 'Sleep on, blest pair' (773)
presents them more like young lovers. But then parents are also

children. There is however a peculiarity about the child-ness of
Milton's Adam and Eve. We see them first as equal adults, lords,
at 288; then as husband and wife; but at 449 Eve tells of her own
'birth' from Adam's rib; it is not until VIII 250 that Adam tells of
his similar waking 'from soundest sleep Soft on the flowery herb
I found me laid In balmy sweat'. In IV then Adam seems adult,
Eve newborn; and born of him. His opened side is typologically
the speared flank of Christ on the cross; psychologically it is a male
vagina; and he too has come from the hands of a male god. The
ultimate ancestry, then, is male. The alternative myth is origin in
the Great Mother. One of the journals of women's liberation is
called *Spare rib* because of the political implications of Milton's
myth. Milton is explicit about the politics. You might collect his
views in IV and add them, for discussion, to some of those in VIII:

> I now see
> Bone of my bone, flesh of my flesh, myself
> Before me; woman is her name, of man
> Extracted.   494

> For well I understand in the prime end
> Of nature her the inferior, in the mind
> And inward faculties, which most excel,
> In outward also her resembling less
> His image who made both.   540

How do you regulate the politics of a marriage? Once again,
Milton projects part of his sexual politics outwards, onto Satan's
'League with you I seek' speech (375), a perverse politicization of
their love. He has the problem of uneven liberation; who hasn't?

G. *Dream*
To reach the organs of her fancy   801

Before reading Eve's dream at V 28 ff, and Christ's at *PR* II 260,
try to collect different *kinds* of dream: You might then look at
Milton's dreams and your own in the light of Freud's *Interpreta-
tion of dreams*. Was Milton correct to distinguish the 'clear dream
and solemn vision' of *Comus* 457 from the post-coital 'grosser
sleep Bred of unkindly fumes, with conscious dreams Encum-
bered' after the fall (IX 1049)? See Isabel MacCaffrey's appendix
to *PL* V in this series, pp. 131–4.

Edwin Muir writes of

> earth's last wonder Eve (the first great dream
> Which is the ground of every dream since then
>
> > *Adam's dream*

So her dream is a dream-within-a-dream; there are implications then for the nature of our reality; or would you rather say that it is we who live in a dream, a false 'spectacle' put on by corporate media, architecture and so on? 'Political organization is theatrical organization, the public realm, where "appearance...constitutes reality" [Hannah Arendt *The human condition*]. To see through this show; to see the invisible reality...' (Brown *Love's body*)

As an *event* Eve's dream is political again. It is she who is first assailed by Satan – the weaker vessel? Yet it is she who manifests the imagination that makes Campbell, in the textbook of human biology cited in the appendix, call man 'the dream animal'. If 'For contemplation he and valour formed', what may be denied the male sex by that political difference? Perhaps it is women who deny it; or perhaps it is Milton who projects onto women certain kinds of experience – such as dreaming – that threaten his masculinity. You may do one of these things in the society you live in.

H. *Communism*

Sole propriety in paradise of all things common else 751

It's unlikely you'll be able to get the members of your group to admit to what they own, and to inequalities of property amongst you. Milton's notion that Adam and Eve possessed each other, but held everything else in common, is strange: can you possess another person? And wasn't God proprietor of the garden? But it points in an interesting direction. Historians tell us so much of the to and fro of battle and debate that they fudge the great ideas that animate people to argue and fight. Christopher Hill is an exception; so was the noble Trevelyan: 'They produced in forms of English thought and speech the great ideas which perished with them, until, after a century and a half, Frenchmen won imperishable honour by making these aspirations the common heritage' (*England under the Stuarts* 1904). But Ashley denies these men political seriousness: theirs is 'a touching faith' (*England in the 17c* Pelican 1952); Davies gives three pages to the 'Putney debates' where these matters were thrashed out, and eleven to the campaign of the first civil war, in the *Early Stuarts* volume of the Oxford History of England (1937). So we have been taught not to notice that during the revolution and the commonwealth of the 1640s and 50s, people did propose pre-Marxist forms of communism and debated them in the equivalent of a revolutionary soviet, the council of the New Model Army in its fortnight's conference at

Putney in October 1647. The steps towards the left in the nation may be represented by Colonel Rainborow the constitutionalist, Lilburne the Leveller and Winstanley the Digger. At Putney Thomas Rainborow argued for manhood suffrage; General Ireton, and Cromwell, argued against him that one-man-one-vote implies the right to equal amounts of property and would produce anarchy. So the vote was seen as a kind of property and the property qualification for voting was fixed at £200; the right to vote was not cleared of property until 1918 (for men over 21; women first had the independent right to vote in 1928). In the country, John Lilburne and the Levellers argued against all inequalities of property and of hierarchy:

That seeing all men are by nature the sons of Adam, and from him have legitimately derived a natural propriety, right and freedom, therefore... ought to be alike free and estated in their natural liberties...and thus the commoners by right are equal with the lords. For by natural birth all men are equally and alike born to like propriety, liberty and freedom...

> Thomas Edwards, a more conservative Presbyterian, reporting in *Gangraena* (cf David Aers' appendix to *PL* VII in this series)

Thirdly Gerrard Winstanley and the Diggers argued not only for equality but for the common use of the actual land by what would now be called 'direct action': 'We have a free right to the land of England, being born therein'; so they aimed (and occasionally started) to cultivate common land and waste land regardless of the wishes of the lords of the manors who controlled it.

Equality is usually projected into utopias (the word means nowhere), either forwards as heaven or backwards as paradise, the Golden Age. They are separated from the present by elaborate *rites de passage* – journeys across rivers and so on. You might try writing equality into your immediate environment as it now is.

I. *Work*

Let us divide our labours

IX 214

It is worth studying Eve's speech there to identify all her arguments, and the anxieties that lie behind them, and those parts of her vocabulary which (like the phrase division of labour) belong to modern usage. For her proposal is the beginning of the fall; yet her arguments are those of industry.

That is not the only paradox. As you will see from the appendix, the sexual division of labour may have been the origin of individuation in the human species; on the other hand, what is 'work' doing in Eden? Even in Book IV you may find the references to it tainted with anxiety; and if they were anxious they were already fallen. (That is in fact one of the standard problems of the fall: how can you fall unless you are already liable to fall, and therefore less than perfect already?)

Milton's failure here raises the problem of what kind of activity would be proper in paradise? Or, to put it the other way round, how do you sanctify work?

J. *The garden*

In narrow room nature's whole wealth 207

The ancient Persian *pairidaeza* was an artificial oasis, a walled pleasure-garden. Its essentials were tree, grass, water, wall; those have remained the essentials of the pleasance, the *locus amoenus* through centuries of European poetry. It is easy to be sentimental about gardens and obvious about oases but difficult to work out exactly what it is that they are for, in life and in literature; even more difficult to see why God should make a garden?

To study this particular garden you might consider some of these characteristics as they recur through Book IV (and if possible V): the language of enclosure, bound, wall, limit; cases of art versus nature; chronographias (epical telling the time); cases of balance, scales, evenness; language that anticipates sin and death (eg yielded, taste...); what are the recurring positive words? (eg sweet, hand?); smells; the language of hair, tangles versus upright, firm; reflections, Narcissus; point of view – whose eyes do you see what through?

Epic similes are a large feature of Book IV and each of them focusses several of those themes. Start with the section on them in *PL: introduction* in this series and then go to the great similes as listed in the contents to this book; pay particular attention to the myths of Persephone and Pandora. Persephone is parallel to Orpheus and Eurydice (*PL: introduction* p. 81); her myth is reworked by Tennyson in *Demeter and Persephone* and by Swinburne in *The garden of Proserpine* and in Stravinsky's oratorio.

You might consider for *PL* as a whole the kind of structure adumbrated by Northrop Frye in *Fables of identity: studies in poetic mythology* (Harcourt Brace 1963) by completing this chart:

creature	unfallen	fallen
man		
animal	flock	
vegetable		forest
mineral		
the unformed	river	flood

K. *The eroticized world*

The mounted sun shone down direct his fervid rays   v 300

Milton perhaps tried to answer some of the awkward questions
raised by paradise partly by letting old Ocean smile and the Sun
shoot invisible virtue even to the deep (III 586): the universe is
animated with erotic delight (cf appendix to *PL* VII in this series,
p. 31). The landscape and especially the garden as a woman's
body was a traditional metaphor (eg 254); but here the whole love
of Adam and Eve is reflected in, and authorized by, their environ-
ment. You will find this enforced also by the description of their
bower; and by their lyrics. Eve's love poem to Adam 639: when
you have analysed the structure into its components (morn,
birds...starry train and back again), consider why it is so strictly
ordered and yet apparently about the sweetness of change? Even-
song 724: compare with the highly structured morning hymn at
v 153.

What would a man-made environment be like that was erotic
in the way that Milton's universe is?

Book III

HAIL, HOLY LIGHT, offspring of heaven first-born,
Or of the eternal co-eternal beam
May I express thee unblamed? since God is light,
And never but in unapproached light
Dwelt from eternity, dwelt then in thee,   5
Bright effluence of bright essence increate.
Or hear'st thou rather pure ethereal stream,
Whose fountain who shall tell? Before the sun,
Before the heavens thou wert, and at the voice
Of God, as with a mantle didst invest   10
The rising world of waters dark and deep,
Won from the void and formless infinite.
Thee I revisit now with bolder wing,
Escaped the Stygian pool, though long detained

1 Hail 'Greetings!' Implies absence, excitement, solemnity of tone.
Contrast with end of II. **Light** M suggests (1) that it was God's first crea-
tion; (2) that it was co-eternal with God; (3) that it is part of the divine
essence although its origin mysterious. All three statements could equally
be applied to the Son's relationship with the Father. But Light is some-
times addressed as a physical rather than a theological entity (see 21ff);
sometimes it seems to be both.   **6 effluence** radiance. **essence** the true
nature of a thing, as opposed to its existence (eg we might say a man leads
a stupid existence but is essentially intelligent). Here it means God,
creator and hence essence of everything. **increate** uncreated; could apply
either to *effluence* or *essence*.   **7 hear'st thou rather** would you rather
be called (Latin construction). **ethereal** heavenly; made of ether, rarefied
atmosphere of the universe beyond the moon's sphere.   **8 Before the
sun...** see VII 243–9 and 354–63 for M's explanation of this.   **10 invest**
wrap (picks up the idea of *mantle*).   **11 The rising world** in VII 232–42
M pictures God forcing the life-giving part of Chaos upward to form the
universe, while the 'dregs adverse to life' sank downwards.   **12 infinite**
Chaos (echoes *Gen.* i).   **13 Thee** Light. **revisit** since he had also ad-
dressed it at beginning of I. **with bolder wing** why? bolder than when he
suggested possible names for it, above, or than when he began poem?
14 Escaped cf I 239 where Satan gloried 'to have scaped the Stygian

In that obscure sojoúrn, while in my flight 15
Through utter and through middle darkness borne
With other notes than to the Orphean lyre
I sung of Chaos and eternal Night,
Taught by the heavenly Muse to venture down
The dark descent, and up to reascend, 20
Though hard and rare: thee I revisit safe,
And feel thy sovereign vital lamp; but thou
Revisit'st not these eyes, that roll in vain
To find thy piercing ray, and find no dawn;
So thick a drop serene hath quenched their orbs, 25
Or dim suffusion veiled. Yet not the more
Cease I to wander where the Muses haunt
Clear spring, or shady grove, or sunny hill,
Smit with the love of sacred song; but chief
Thee Sion and the flowery brooks beneath 30
That wash thy hallowed feet, and warbling flow,
Nightly I visit: nor sometimes forget

flood' by his own strength alone. **Stygian** gloomy, like river Styx at
entrance to classical underworld. **15 obscure** dark. **sojoúrn** tem-
porary dwelling. **16 utter and...middle darkness** hell and Chaos.
17 other notes unlike (and perhaps better than?) those of Orpheus, who
also returned safely from an underworld journey, but whose song was a
lament for the loss of his wife Eurydice. **21 hard and rare** the upward
journey; echoes the Sibyl's warning to Aeneas that anyone can descend to
the underworld; the problem is to get out again. **thee** Light; M is picking
up the threads from 13; notice how the long intervening passage imitates
the sense of being 'long detained'. **22 sovereign vital** supremely life-
giving; could be said of a medicine, which adds to the paradoxes of this
passage, already implied in the repetition of *revisit*. Pronounce *sovran*,
which is how M spelled it. **25 drop serene** and **dim suffusion** sound
poetic but translate contemporary medical terms for blindness, *gutta
serena* and *suffusio nigra*. **26 Yet not the more...** what does M gain by
using the multiple negatives? Literally, the passage means that, despite
his blindness he continues to keep in touch with great poetry, especially
that of the Hebrew Bible (**Sion**, or Zion, is the hill in Jerusalem on which
the Temple was built; Milton contrasts it with Helicon, the mountain in
Greece which was sacred to the classical **muses**, patrons of the various
arts). The imagery is reminiscent of *Il penseroso*: night, solitude, the
nightingale, poetry, contemplation. **30 flowery brooks** Shiloh –
again, a Hebrew counterpart to the Greek Aganippe, well of the muses.
32 Nightly both because it is always night for a blind man and because M
did in fact compose much of *PL* by night, dictating to a scribe early next
morning. **nor sometimes forget** and often remember.

Those other two equalled with me in fate,
So were I equalled with them in renown,
Blind Thámyris, and blind Maeónides,   35
And Tirésias and Phíneus prophets old.
Then feed on thoughts, that voluntary move
Harmonious numbers; as the wakeful bird
Sings darkling, and in shadiest covert hid
Tunes her nocturnal note. Thus with the year   40
Seasons return, but not to me returns
Day, or the sweet approach of even or morn,
Or sight of vernal bloom, or summer's rose,
Or flocks, or herds, or human face divine;
But cloud in stead, and ever-during dark   45
Surrounds me, from the cheerful ways of men
Cut off, and for the book of knowledge fair
Presented with a universal blank
Of nature's works to me expunged and razed,
And wisdom at one entrance quite shut out.   50
So much the rather thou celestial Light
Shine inward, and the mind through all her powers
Irradiate, there plant eyes, all mist from thence
Purge and disperse, that I may see and tell
Of things invisible to mortal sight.   55

34 So were I if only I were like them in fame as I am in blindness.   **35
Thámyris** a poet, blinded as a punishment for falling in love with the
muses and challenging them to a singing contest (cf M's ' smit with the love
of sacred song'). **Maeónides** Homer (his blindness is a tradition rather than
a fact). **36 Tirésias** prophet who frequently appears in Greek drama (eg
Sophocles' *Oedipus*) and is the central figure of Eliot's *Waste Land*. **Phíneus**
a Thracian king, also blind and a prophet.   **37 feed** goes with 'I' of
previous sentence. **voluntary** both an adjective with **numbers** and an
adverb with **move** – may also suggest improvised music, as 'an organ
voluntary'.   **38 bird** nightingale.   **39 darkling** in the dark; Keats
uses this word in *Ode to nightingale* but connotations more 'poetic' for
him than for M. **covert** hiding place.   **41ff** Notice the effect of repeated
or.   **43 vernal** springtime.   **44 human face divine** sandwiching a
noun between two adjectives is a Latin trick; what's the effect here?
46 *Cut off* goes with *me*; the line break between them emphasizes the
deprivation.   **47 book of knowledge** nature, traditionally compared
to a book written by God.   **48 blank...expunged and razed** blank
page and blank universe, as if the outer world had been sponged off a
blackboard.   **50 entrance** of the senses, ie sight.

Now had the almighty Father from above,
From the pure empýreän where he sits
High throned above all highth, bent down his eye,
His own works and their works at once to view:
About him all the sanctities of heaven   60
Stood thick as stars, and from his sight received
Beatitude past utterance; on his right
The radiant image of his glory sat,
His only Son; on earth he first beheld
Our two first parents, yet the only two   65
Of mankind, in the happy garden placed,
Reaping immortal fruits of joy and love,
Uninterrupted joy, unrivalled love
In blissful solitude; he then surveyed
Hell and the gulf between, and Satan there   70
Coasting the wall of heaven on this side night
In the dun air sublime, and ready now
To stoop with wearied wings, and willing feet,
On the bare outside of this world, that seemed
Firm land imbosomed without firmament,   75
Uncertain which, in ocean or in air.
Him God beholding from his prospect high,
Wherein past, present, future he beholds,
Thus to his only Son foreseeing spake.

   'Only begotten Son, seest thou what rage   80
Transports our adversary, whom no bounds
Prescribed, no bars of hell, nor all the chains

56 Now 'meanwhile'? not exactly; one effect of this word is to remind us
that God exists in an eternal present tense. Notice how the language
underlines this.   **57 empýreän** the highest heaven.   **59 works** both
the angels and man.   **60 sanctities** angels.   **65 yet** still, so far.
67 immortal fruits!   71 Coasting 'along' understood. **on this side
night** the side of Chaos closest to heaven.   **72 dun** dark. **sublime** aloft.
75 Firm land...without firmament   God's view of Satan includes a
vision of the world as Satan sees it; the outer shell of the universe, really
only a hollow case for the moving spheres, looks to S like solid land.
76 Uncertain because Chaos is neither one thing nor the other – again,
God takes a Satan's-eye-view.   **81 Transports** pun, depending on
literal and metaphorical meanings of the word. **adversary** literal trans-
lation of Satan.

Heaped on him there, nor yet the main abyss
Wide interrupt can hold; so bent he seems
On desperate revenge, that shall redound   85
Upon his own rebellious head. And now
Through all restraint broke loose he wings his way
Not far off heaven, in the precincts of light,
Directly towards the new created world,
And man there placed, with purpose to assay   90
If him by force he can destroy, or worse,
By some false guile pervert; and shall pervert
For man will hearken to his glozing lies,
And easily transgress the sole command,
Sole pledge of his obedience: so will fall,   95
He and his faithless progeny: whose fault?
Whose but his own? Ingrate, he had of me
All he could have; I made him just and right,
Sufficient to have stood, though free to fall.
Such I created all the ethereal powers   100
And spirits, both them who stood and them who failed;
Freely they stood who stood, and fell who fell.
Not free, what proof could they have given sincere
Of true allegiance, constant faith or love,
Where only what they needs must do, appeared,   105
Not what they would? What praise could they receive?
What pleasure I from such obedience paid,
When will and reason (reason also is choice)
Useless and vain, of freedom both despoiled,
Made passive both, had served necessity,   110

83 **abyss** Chaos, cutting off hell from the universe (an effect imitated by
the strategic line-break).   88 **precincts** the area surrounding God
who = light.   90 **assay** test. Grammatically, as well as logically, both
God and Satan are described as testing man.   92 **pervert** turn from his
rightful direction (cf convert: to turn to God). In reading, stress *shall*, and
notice the speed of this passage, mirroring both Satan's arrow-like flight
and the rapidity of man's fall, also God's timeless vision in which future
events are seen as present.   93 **glozing** flattering.   97 **Ingrate** un-
grateful.   107 **What pleasure I** what pleasure could *I* receive? A typical
example of God's compressed style.   109 **Useless and vain** unused
and empty, existing in name only.   110 **necessity** fate.

Not me. They therefore as to right belonged,
So were created, nor can justly accuse
Their maker, or their making, or their fate,
As if predestination overruled
Their will, disposed by absolute decree   115
Or high foreknowledge; they themselves decreed
Their own revolt, not I: if I foreknew,
Foreknowledge had no influence on their fault,
Which had no less proved certain unforeknown.
So without least impulse or shadow of fate,   120
Or aught by me immutably foreseen,
They trespass, authors to themselves in all
Both what they judge and what they choose; for so
I formed them free, and free they must remain,
Till they enthrall themselves: I else must change   125
Their nature, and revoke the high decree
Unchangeable, eternal, which ordained
Their freedom, they themselves ordained their fall.
The first sort by their own suggestion fell,
Self-tempted, self-depraved: man falls deceived   130
By the other first: man therefore shall find grace,
The other none: in mercy and justice both,
Through heaven and earth, so shall my glory excel,
But mercy first and last shall brightest shine.'

        Thus while God spake, ambrosial fragrance filled   135
All heaven, and in the blessed spirits elect
Sense of new joy ineffable diffused:
Beyond compare the Son of God was seen
Most glorious, in him all his Father shone
Substantially expressed, and in his face   140

112 So ie free and rational.   **114 predestination** see introduction.
125 else otherwise.   **129 first sort** the angels. **suggestion** temptation.
135 ambrosial like ambrosia, food of the Homeric gods. This description
of one sense in terms of another, so that God's words smell rather than
sound, is called synesthesia; it's more frequently found in 19c poets.
136 elect chosen by God to salvation, but (here M differs from Calvinists)
chosen as a result of their own free choice to remain with God.   **137
ineffable** inexpressible.   **140 Substantially expressed** as a visible

Divine compassion visibly appeared,
Love without end, and without measure grace,
Which uttering thus he to his Father spake.
  'O Father, gracious was that word which closed
Thy sovereign sentence, that man should find grace;   145
For which both heaven and earth shall high extol
Thy praises, with the innumerable sound
Of hymns and sacred songs, wherewith thy throne
Encompassed shall resound thee ever blessed.
For should man finally be lost, should man   150
Thy creature late so loved, thy youngest son
Fall circumvented thus by fraud, though joined
With his own folly? That be from thee far,
That far be from thee, Father, who art judge
Of all things made, and judgest only right.   155
Or shall the adversary thus obtain
His end, and frustrate thine, shall he fulfil
His malice, and thy goodness bring to nought,
Or proud return though to his heavier doom,
Yet with revenge accomplished and to hell   160
Draw after him the whole race of mankind,
By his corrupted? Or wilt thou thy self
Abolish thy creation, and unmake,
For him, what for thy glory thou hast made?
So should thy goodness and thy greatness both   165
Be questioned and blasphemed without defence.'
  To whom the great creator thus replied.
'O Son, in whom my soul hath chief delight,
Son of my bosom, Son who art alone
My word, my wisdom, and effectual might,   170
All hast thou spoken as my thoughts are, all
As my eternal purpose hath decreed:

substance – unlike God, who is invisible and insubstantial. **142** Notice
rhythm and rhyme, and cf speeches which precede and follow. **146**
high both highly and high in heaven. **149 resound** echoing *sound* in
147. Onomatopoeic effects all through here. **151 late** refers both to
time of man's creation and to the fact that God lately loved him. **152**
fraud how does the Son's way of describing man's fall differ from God's?
162 his his race of devils. **164 him** Satan.

Man shall not quite be lost, but saved who will,
Yet not of will in him, but grace in me
Freely vouchsafed; once more I will renew   175
His lapsèd powers, though forfeit and enthralled
By sin to foul exorbitant desires;
Upheld by me, yet once more he shall stand
On even ground against his mortal foe,
By me upheld, that he may know how frail   180
His fallen condition is, and to me owe
All his deliverance, and to none but me.
Some I have chosen of peculiar grace
Elect above the rest; so is my will:
The rest shall hear me call, and oft be warned   185
Their sinful state, and to appease betimes
The incensèd Deity, while offered grace
Invites; for I will clear their senses dark,
What may suffice, and soften stony hearts
To pray, repent, and bring obedience due.   190
To prayer, repentance, and obedience due,
Though but endeavoured with sincere intent,
Mine ear shall not be slow, mine eye not shut.
And I will place within them as a guide
My umpire conscience, whom if they will hear,   195
Light after light well used they shall attain,
And to the end persisting, safe arrive.
This my long sufferance and my day of grace
They who neglect and scorn, shall never taste;
But hard be hardened, blind be blinded more,   200

176 lapsèd fallen in both senses. **forfeit** legal terminology. The idea is
that God's grace will give man strength to resist his own passions, which,
because of sin, would otherwise be too powerful for him.   **183 peculiar
grace** contrasted with *sufficient* grace (III 99) which is granted to everyone.
186 betimes early.   **187 incensèd** angry – but possible pun here,
because the prayers which would appease God are often compared to
incense.   **196 Light after light** if they follow conscience, they will
attain light and, if they use that well, further light.   **200 hardened**
and **blinded** the opposite of *clear* and *soften* in 188–9. The Bible often
describes God as 'hardening' men's hearts (NEB: 'making them stub-
born'), but M insists that this only happens to those who are 'hard'
already.

That they may stumble on, and deeper fall;
And none but such from mercy I exclude.
But yet all is not done; man disobeying,
Disloyal breaks his fealty, and sins
Against the high supremacy of heaven,   205
Affecting Godhead, and so losing all,
To expiate his treason hath nought left,
But to destruction sacred and devote,
He with his whole posterity must die,
Die he or justice must; unless for him   210
Some other able, and as willing, pay
The rigid satisfaction, death for death.
Say heavenly powers, where shall we find such love,
Which of ye will be mortal to redeem
Man's mortal crime, and just the unjust to save,   215
Dwells in all heaven charity so dear?'

    He asked, but all the heavenly choir stood mute,
And silence was in heaven: on man's behalf
Patron or intercessor none appeared,
Much less that durst upon his own head draw   220
The deadly forfeiture, and ransom set.
And now without redemption all mankind
Must have been lost, adjudged to death and hell
By doom severe, had not the Son of God,
In whom the fulness dwells of love divine,   225
His dearest mediation thus renewed.

    'Father, thy word is past, man shall find grace;
And shall Grace not find means, that finds her way,
The speediest of thy wingèd messengers,
To visit all thy creatures, and to all   230

204 **fealty** again, legal: allegiance.   206 **Affecting** aspiring to.   208
devote doomed. Man is now serving death instead of God; in a sense, he's
a human sacrifice, which is why another human sacrifice is required to take
his place.   214 **mortal** first 'capable of dying' then 'deadly'. Similar
double meanings throughout.   216 **dear** both beloved and costly (thus
carrying on financial language).   224 **doom** judgment.   227 **word**
promise.

Comes unprevented, unimplored, unsought,
Happy for man, so coming; he her aid
Can never seek, once dead in sins and lost;
Atonement for himself or offering meet,
Indebted and undone, hath none to bring: 235
Behold me then, me for him, life for life
I offer, on me let thine anger fall;
Account me man; I for his sake will leave
Thy bosom, and this glory next to thee
Freely put off, and for him lastly die   240
Well pleased, on me let Death wreak all his rage;
Under his gloomy power I shall not long
Lie vanquished; thou hast given me to possess
Life in my self for ever, by thee I live,
Though now to Death I yield, and am his due   245
All that of me can die, yet that debt paid,
Thou wilt not leave me in the loathsome grave
His prey, nor suffer my unspotted soul
For ever with corruption there to dwell;
But I shall rise victorious, and subdue   250
My vanquisher, spoiled of his vaunted spoil;
Death his death's wound shall then receive, and stoop
Inglorious, of his mortal sting disarmed.
I through the ample air in triumph high
Shall lead hell captive maugrë hell, and show   255
The powers of darkness bound. Thou at the sight
Pleased, out of heaven shalt look down and smile,
While by thee raised I ruin all my foes,
Death last, and with his carcass glut the grave:
Then with the multitude of my redeemed   260
Shall enter heaven long absent, and return,
Father, to see thy face, wherein no cloud

231 **unprevented** ie man can't meet it halfway.   **232 Happy**
fortunate.   **234 meet** appropriate. This whole phrase is the object
of '[he] hath' in next line.   **251 spoiled** another play on words,
reflecting theme of beating death with its own weapons.   **255 maugrë**
in spite of (Fr. *malgré*).   **258 ruin** throw down.   **261 long absent**
from which I've been long absent.

Of anger shall remain, but peace assured,
And reconcilement; wrath shall be no more
Thenceforth, but in thy presence joy entire.'   265

  His words here ended, but his meek aspéct
Silent yet spake, and breathed immortal love
To mortal men, above which only shone
Filial obedience: as a sacrifice
Glad to be offered, he attends the will   270
Of his great Father. Admiration seized
All heaven, what this might mean, and whither tend
Wondering; but soon the almighty thus replied:
  'O thou in heaven and earth the only peace
Found out for mankind under wrath, O thou   270
My sole complacence! well thou know'st how dear
To me are all my works, nor man the least
Though last created, that for him I spare
Thee from my bosom and right hand, to save,
By losing thee awhile, the whole race lost.   280
Thou therefore whom thou only canst redeem,
Their nature also to thy nature join;
And be thy self man among men on earth,
Made flesh, when time shall be, of virgin seed,
By wondrous birth: be thou in Adam's room   285
The head of all mankind, though Adam's son.
As in him perish all men, so in thee
As from a second root shall be restored,
As many as are restored, without thee none.
His crime makes guilty all his sons, thy merit   290
Imputed shall absolve them who renounce
Their own both righteous and unrighteous deeds,

---

270 attends awaits; note switch to present and timeless. **271 Admira-
tion** wonder (but modern meaning also applies). **276 complacence**
pleasure. **281** Loose syntax; probably means 'join to thine the nature
of those whom thou only canst redeem', but M may also imply that the
Son in his human role can be redeemed only by himself. **285 room**
place. **288 root** goes with *seed* (284) – an image based on *Gen*. iii,
transplanted (293), *fruition* (307) and *fruitful* (337). **291 Imputed** de-
rived at second hand. **292 righteous and unrighteous** man must do

And live in thee transplanted, and from thee
Receive new life. So man, as is most just,
Shall satisfy for man, be judged and die,   295
And dying rise, and rising with him raise
His brethren, ransomed with his own dear life.
So heavenly love shall outdo hellish hate
Giving to death, and dying to redeem,
So dearly to redeem what hellish hate   300
So easily destroyed, and still destroys
In those who, when they may, accept not grace.
Nor shalt thou by descending to assume
Man's nature, lessen or degrade thine own.
Because thou hast, though throned in highest bliss   305
Equal to God, and equally enjoying
Godlike fruition, quitted all to save
A world from utter loss, and hast been found
By merit more than birthright Son of God,
Found worthiest to be so by being good,   310
Far more than great or high; because in thee
Love hath abounded more than glory abounds,
Therefore thy humiliation shall exalt
With thee thy manhood also to this throne,
Here shalt thou sit incarnate, here shalt reign   315
Both God and man, Son both of God and man,
Anointed universal king, all power
I give thee, reign for ever, and assume
Thy merits; under thee as head supreme
Thrones, princedoms, powers, dominions I reduce: 320
All knees to thee shall bow, of them that bide

good works but not expect to be saved by anything but God alone.   **294–
302** In reading, bring out the pattern here.   **299 Giving** the subject
is love (represented by both Father and Son); it contrasts with *redeem*,
which means buy back, and *dearly* refers to the price.   **307 Godlike
fruition** another pun on *fruit*. **quitted** both left (all = the Son's power
and glory in heaven) and atoned (all = man's debt of sin and death).
309 By merit some advocates of predestination argued that it applied
even in heaven and that the Son was exalted above the other angels be-
cause God foreknew his actions; but M clearly means that this exaltation
was *earned*, foreknown or not.   **315 incarnate** in the flesh.   **318 I
give thee** present and future. **assume** take possession of.

In heaven, or earth, or under earth in hell,
When thou attended gloriously from heaven
Shalt in the sky appear, and from thee send
The summoning archangels to proclaim   325
Thy dread tribunal: forthwith from all winds
The living, and forthwith the cited dead
Of all past ages to the general doom
Shall hasten, such a peal shall rouse their sleep.
Then, all thy saints assembled, thou shalt judge   330
Bad men and angels, they arraigned shall sink
Beneath thy sentence; hell, her numbers full,
Thenceforth shall be for ever shut. Mean while
The world shall burn, and from her ashes spring
New heaven and earth, wherein the just shall dwell,   335
And after all their tribulations long
See golden days, fruitful of golden deeds,
With joy and love triúmphing, and fair truth.
Then thou thy regal sceptre shalt lay by,
For regal sceptre then no more shall need,   340
God shall be all in all. But all ye gods,
Adore him, who to compass all this dies,
Adore the Son, and honour him as me.'

No sooner had the almighty ceased, but all
The multitude of angels with a shout   345
Loud as from numbers without number, sweet
As from blest voices, uttering joy, heaven rung
With jubilee, and loud hosannas filled
The eternal regions: lowly reverent
Towards either throne they bow, and to the ground   350

323 attended awaited or accompanied; **gloriously** can refer either
to *attended* or *appear*. The whole passage heavily based on *Revela-
tion*.   **326 all winds** all corners of the earth (see Donne's *Holy
sonnet* vii).   **327 cited** summoned.   **328 general doom** last judg-
ment.   **330 assembled** when the blessed souls have been assembled.
340 shall need shall be needed.   **341 gods** angels sometimes called
gods in Bible.   **346 numbers** play on words: could mean music.   **347
rung** the shout rang heaven? Very loose structure here; could be a series
of afterthoughts.

With solemn adoration down they cast
Their crowns inwove with amarant and gold,
Immortal amarant, a flower which once
In paradise, fast by the tree of life
Began to bloom, but soon for man's offence   355
To heaven removed where first it grew, there grows,
And flowers aloft shading the fount of life,
And where the river of bliss through midst of heaven
Rolls o'er Elysian flowers her amber stream;
With these that never fade the spirits elect   360
Bind their resplendent locks inwreathed with beams,
Now in loose garlands thick thrown off, the bright
Pavement that like a sea of jasper shone
Impurpled with celestial roses smiled.
Then crowned again their golden harps they took,   365
Harps ever tuned, that glittering by their side
Like quivers hung, and with preamble sweet
Of charming symphony they introduce
Their sacred song, and waken raptures high;
No voice exempt, no voice but well could join   370

352–61 Long parenthesis explaining about the crowns. **amarant**
a purple flower, symbolized immortality and was also used to deck
the hearse in *Lyc*.   **355 for** because of. Shifting tense – began,
soon, removed, grew, grows – makes immortal amarant seem to
have no beginning or end.   **357f. fount** and **river** universal images of
earthly and heavenly paradise. One can see why: water = source of life
(sexual imagery) and is literal salvation in desert country.   **359 Elysian**
The Elysian fields were the happiest part of the classical afterlife: a curious
reference here?   **amber** partly a visual and tactile comparison, but may
also be symbolic, as amber does preserve things.   **360 these** their
crowns and the amarant flowers.   **361 inwreathed** the angels really
have a triple wreath or crown: their shining hair, their halos, and the
garlands.   **362 thick** the pavement is thick with flowers (as the fallen
angels lay on the burning lake 'thick as autumnal leaves' I 302).   **364**
The pavement smiles figuratively in a riot of roses. Similarly, Raphael is
said to give 'a smile that glowed Celestial rosy red, love's proper hue'
(VIII 619).   **367 quivers** because of the shape and because they're al-
ways ready for use like arrows.   **368 symphony** in 17c = a short instru-
mental introduction. Comes from Greek word for concord. **charming**
probably used in strongest sense; it derives ultimately from *carmen*,
which also means song.   **370 exempt** left out. *All* the angels can do
what many people in M's time could do: join in elaborate, unrehearsed
part-song.

Melodious part, such concord is in heaven.
  Thee Father first they sung omnipotent,
Immutable, immortal, infinite.
Eternal king; thee author of all being,
Fountain of light, thy self invisible   375
Amidst the glorious brightness where thou sit'st
Throned inaccessible, but when thou shadest
The full blaze of thy beams, and through a cloud
Drawn round about thee like a radiant shrine,
Dark with excessive bright thy skirts appear,   380
Yet dazzle heaven, that brightest seraphim
Approach not, but with both wings veil their eyes.
Thee next they sang of all creation first,
Begotten Son, divine similitude,
In whose conspicuous countenance, without cloud   385
Made visible, the almighty Father shines,
Whom else no creature can behold; on thee
Impressed the effulgence of his glory abides,
Transfused on thee his ample Spirit rests.
He heaven of heavens and all the powers therein   390
By thee created, and by thee threw down
The aspiring dominations: thou that day
Thy Father's dreadful thunder didst not spare,
Nor stop thy flaming chariot wheels, that shook
Heaven's everlasting frame, while o'er the necks   395
Thou drovest of warring angels disarrayed.
Back from pursuit thy powers with loud acclaim

377 **but** except.   380 **skirts** outermost edge of God's radiance.
381 **seraphim** chief of the 9 orders of angels, devoted to love
and hence usually depicted as red and burning.   383 **first** in time
and in power.   384 **similitude** image of God made visible.   385
conspicuous clearly visible.   387 **else no creature** ambiguous: either
'no creature can behold except through the Son' or 'no creature except
the Son can behold'.   390 **heaven of heavens** M is following a Hebrew
distinction between heaven (the sky) and the dwelling place of God,
placed in the highest of 7 heavens.   392 **dominations** one of the 9
orders of angels, but used by M interchangeably with seraph, cherub, etc;
the rebel angels came from all ranks.   393 **didst not spare** negatives
emphasized, to contrast with the mercy the Son will show to man.   396
disarrayed in confusion; array usually means line-up for battle.

Thee only extolled, Son of thy Father's might,
To execute fierce vengeance on his foes,
Not so on man; him through their malice fallen, 400
Father of mercy and grace, thou didst not doom
So strictly, but much more to pity incline:
No sooner did thy dear and only Son
Perceive thee purposed not to doom frail man
So strictly, but much more to pity inclined, 405
He to appease thy wrath, and end the strife
Of mercy and justice in thy face discerned,
Regardless of the bliss wherein he sat
Second to thee, offered himself to die
For man's offence. O unexampled love, 410
Love nowhere to be found less than divine!
Hail, Son of God, saviour of men, thy name
Shall be the copious matter of my song
Henceforth, and never shall my harp thy praise
Forget, nor from thy Father's praise disjoin. 415
 Thus they in heaven, above the starry sphere,
Their happy hours in joy and hymning spent.

Mean while upon the firm opacous globe
Of this round world, whose first convéx divides
The luminous inferior orbs, enclosed 420
From Chaos and the inroad of darkness old,
Satan alighted walks: a globe far off
It seemed, now seems a boundless continent
Dark, waste, and wild, under the frown of Night

403 Effect of this repetition? 406 Some morality plays actually depicted
the strife of Mercy and Justice for man's soul (see *The castle of perseve-
rance* 15c). But is the image of internal strife appropriate to God himself?
408 **Regardless** disregarding. 412 **Hail** echoes opening of III, also
emphasizes that the Son has passed a sort of test and proved himself
worthy to be praised in the same breath as the Father. 416 **sphere**
farthest visible bound of the universe. The stars were thought to be nailed
into their sphere, beyond the planets and just inside the *primum mobile*
which turned them all at once. Compare this summary with 'the irksome
hours' of the rebel angels (II 522–7) and 'the fruitless hours' of Adam and
Eve's 'mutual accusation' (IX 1187–9). 418–21 As in II 1–5, Satan's
name is delayed; what's the effect? 424ff The references to Chaos,

Starless exposed, and ever-threatening storms   425
Of Chaos blustering round, inclement sky;
Save on that side which from the wall of heaven
Though distant far some small reflection gains
Of glimmering air less vexed with tempest loud:
Here walked the fiend at large in spacious field.   430
As when a vulture on Imáus bred,
Whose snowy ridge the roving Tartar bounds,
Dislodging from a region scarce of prey
To gorge the flesh of lambs or yeanling kids
On hills where flocks are fed, flies toward the springs   435
Of Ganges or Hydáspes, Indian streams;
But in his way lights on the barren plains
Of Sericána, where Chineses drive
With sails and wind their cany wagons light:
So on this windy sea of land, the fiend   440
Walked up and down alone bent on his prey,
Alone, for other creature in this place
Living or lifeless to be found was none,
None yet, but store hereafter from the earth
Up hither like aërial vapours flew   445
Of all things transitory and vain, when sin
With vanity had filled the works of men:
Both all things vain, and all who in vain things
Built their fond hopes of glory or lasting fame,
Or happiness in this or the other life;   450
All who have their reward on earth, the fruits

darkness, and reflected light from heaven are moral as well as physical.
430 at large pun.   **431–9** See preface and introduction. **Sericána** was
in northwest China; **Imáus** a mountain range in what is now Afghanistan;
Tartars were traditionally thought of as wicked and deceitful, so this pas-
sage continues 'barbarian' images of I 351–5, while *vulture* points to *cor-
morant* in IV 194–6. Vultures were supposed to be hermaphrodites and
their eggs were believed to be fertilized by the wind: a link with the
allegory of the paradise of fools.   **444 None yet** change of tone: an
afterthought, setting this satiric passage off from its context. **store** enough
to fill the place.   **447 vanith** both conceit and emptiness.   **449 fond**
foolish.   **451 reward on earth** echoes Christ's description of hypo-
crites (*Matt.* vi) and is aimed at Roman catholic belief that good works
could contribute to man's salvation.

Of painful superstition and blind zeal,
Nought seeking but the praise of men, here find
Fit retribution, empty as their deeds;
All the unaccomplished works of nature's hand,   455
Abortive, monstrous, or unkindly mixed,
Dissolved on earth, fleet hither, and in vain,
Till final dissolution, wander here,
Not in the neighbouring moon, as some have dreamed;
Those argent fields more likely habitants,   460
Translated saints, or middle spirits hold
Betwixt the angelical and human kind:
Hither of ill-joined sons and daughters born
First from the ancient world those giants came
With many a vain exploit, though then renowned: 465
The builders next of Babel on the plain
Of Sennaär, and still with vain design
New Babels, had they wherewithal, would build.
Others came single; he who to be deemed
A god, leaped fondly into Aetna flames,   470
Empédocles, and he who to enjoy

455 unaccomplished incomplete, imperfect; these are all works of nature – human freaks – but their own works are also described as vain. **456 unkindly** unnaturally: eg the giants, who were supposed to be offspring of 'the sons of God' and 'the daughters of men'; see *Gen.* vi. **457 in vain** pun: uselessly and in emptiness. **458 final dissolution** M believed that the soul died with the body and was resurrected with it at the last judgment rather than surviving on its own; thus the damned died twice. For the purposes of his fantasy, he gives the fools a ghostlike existence after death. **459** A back-handed acknowledgment of his debt to Ariosto and other authors of voyages to the moon. **461 Translated saints** the Bible gives three examples: Enoch, who 'walked with God', Elijah, who ascended in a fiery chariot, and possibly the disciple John, to whom Christ seems to have promised freedom from death (see *Genesis* v, *II Kings* ii, and *John* xxi). The structure here is 'fields…hold…habitants…eg saints etc'. **464** The giants were destroyed in the flood and their deeds forgotten. Many peoples have a legend about a larger, stronger race which preceded theirs. **466–8** 'Came' is understood. The Babel story is a myth to explain why men speak so many different languages. Sometimes it got a reformation interpretation: the different sects of protestantism were a punishment for Roman catholic ambition. Hence line 468. **471 Empédocles** a Greek philosopher; M sees him as a parody of the translated saints (legend said that the smoke from Etna blew him up to the moon), but Matthew Arnold's *Empedocles on Etna* gives a less cynical view of his suicide.

Plato's Elysium, leaped into the sea,
Cleómbrotus, and many more too long,
Embryos and idiots, eremites and friars
White, black and gray, with all their trumpery.   475
Here pilgrims roam, that strayed so far to seek
In Golgotha him dead, who lives in heaven;
And they who to be sure of paradise
Dying put on the weeds of Dominic,
Or in Franciscan think to pass disguised;   480
They pass the planets seven, and pass the fixed,
And that crystálline sphere whose balance weighs
The trepidation talked, and that first moved;
And now Saint Peter at heaven's wicket seems
To wait them with his keys, and now at foot   485
Of heaven's ascent they lift their feet, when lo
A violent cross wind from either coast
Blows them transverse ten thousand leagues awry

473 Cleómbrotus all that's known about him is what M says;
what's the effect of putting his name, and Empedocles', at the *end* of his
description? **too long** too many to mention.   **474 Embryos and idiots**
the Roman catholic belief that these existed in limbo was a way of
avoiding the full horror of the doctrine that unbaptized infants couldn't
go to heaven. **eremites** hermits – examples of the 'fugitive and cloistered
virtue' which M condemns in *Areopagitica*. Archimago, the villain of
Spenser's *Fairy queen*, is disguised as a hermit; so is Satan in *PR*.   **475
White, black and gray** Carmelites, Dominicans and Franciscans respec-
tively. Blackfriars in London was once the site of a Dominican monastery.
trumpery theatrical costume or trashy clothes.   **477 Golgotha** where
Christ was crucified; M always refuses to believe that any place is in-
trinsically holy – cf *PL* XI 334–54 and 829–38.   **481 fixed** the 'starry
sphere' of III 416; the planets were sometimes called 'wandering stars' in
contrast. In reading, make the most of all the 'ands' in this passage,
building up a sarcastic mock-suspense until 'lo' in 486.   **482–3 crystál-
line** there was no visible evidence of this sphere so it was assumed to be
transparent. Astronomers postulated its existence to explain the **trepida-
tion talked** ('the so-called trepidation') which Donne mentions in
Valediction forbidding mourning. See Astronomy in introduction. **first
moved** the *primum mobile*, tenth and outermost sphere of the universe
which moved all the others.   **485 wait** both await and wait on. St Peter
is reduced to the role of a porter, rather as in Byron's *Vision of judgment*,
but *seems to* shows that this is only happening in the deluded minds of
Roman catholic souls.   **485–6 foot** and **feet** a pun or just carelessness?
heaven's ascent the golden stairway described below, 501–22, at
precisely the opposite side of the universe.   **488 transverse** sideways.

Into the devious air; then might ye see
Cowls, hoods and habits with their wearers tossed   490
And fluttered into rags, then relics, beads,
Indulgences, dispenses, pardons, bulls,
The sport of winds: all these upwhirled aloft
Fly o'er the backside of the world far off
Into a limbo large and broad, since called   495
The Paradise of Fools, to few unknown
Long after, now unpeopled, and untrod.

All this dark globe the fiend found as he passed,
And long he wandered, till at last a gleam
Of dawning light turned thitherward in haste   500
His travelled steps; far distant he descries,
Ascending by degrees magnificent
Up to the wall of heaven a structure high,
At top whereof, but far more rich appeared
The work as of a kingly palace gate   505
With frontispiece of diamond and gold
Embellished, thick with sparkling orient gems
The portal shone, inimitable on earth
By model, or by shading pencil drawn.
The stairs were such as whereon Jacob saw   510

489 devious both off-course and deceitful. **492** Series of devices by
which catholics thought salvation could be earned: **Indulgences** partial
remission of punishment in purgatory in exchange for prayers, good works
or (in pre-reformation times) money. **dispenses** papal dispensations from
legal obligations. **bulls** papal proclamations, so called because fastened
with a *bulla* or seal. **494 backside** deliberately vulgar, especially com-
bined with the winds of 493. The front side of the universe is the one
turned toward heaven. **495 since** in future times. M generally uses
this word to jolt us into or out of the time scheme of his poem. **496
Paradise of Fools** proverbial expression for delusion. Eg the Nurse in
Romeo and Juliet warns Romeo 'if you should lead her in a fool's paradise,
as they say, it were a very gross kind of behaviour, as they say' (II iv).
501 travelled weary with travel. **502 degrees** steps. **504 more
rich** than the stairs? than the palace gate to which it's compared? **506
frontispiece** decoration on or over the entrance. **507 orient** both
lustrous (a technical term applied to pearls) and eastern. East usually =
God as north = Satan. **510** The implication of **such** is that the ladder
of Jacob's vision was *like* this one, but not necessarily the same.

Angels ascending and descending, bands
Of guardians bright, when he from Esau fled
To Pádan-Áram, in the field of Luz
Dreaming by night under the open sky,
And waking cried, 'This is the gate of heaven.'   515
Each stair mysteriously was meant, nor stood
There always, but drawn up to heaven sometimes
Viewless, and underneath a bright sea flowed
Of jasper, or of liquid pearl, whereon
Who after came from earth, sailing arrived,   520
Wafted by angels, or flew o'er the lake
Rapt in a chariot drawn by fiery steeds.
The stairs were then let down, whether to dare
The fiend by easy ascent, or aggravate
His sad exclusion from the doors of bliss.   525
Direct against which opened from beneath,
Just o'er the blissful seat of paradise,
A passage down to the earth, a passage wide,
Wider by far than that of after-times
Over Mount Sion, and, though that were large,   530
Over the Promised Land to God so dear,
By which, to visit oft those happy tribes,
On high behests his angels to and fro
Passed frequent, and his eye with choice regard
From Páneas the fount of Jordan's flood   535
To Bëërsaba, where the Holy Land
Borders on Egypt and the Arabian shore;
So wide the opening seemed, where bounds were set
To darkness, such as bound the ocean wave.

516 was meant had a **mysterious** (symbolic) meaning.   **518** The **bright
sea**, as M explains in his 'argument', is identified with the waters above
the earth which are mentioned in *Gen*. i. The references to precious stones
come from *Rev*. A counterpart to the fiery lake of hell.   **524 aggravate**
intensify.   **528 passage wide** because it gets a lot of use; after the fall
angelic visits will be less frequent and the passage more narrow. An
allegory.   **534 frequent** both frequently and in large numbers. **Passed**
goes with both *angels* and *eye*.   **535-9 Páneas** another name for Dan:
'from Dan to Beersheba' was a common biblical expression for 'the
length of the Holy Land'. As Israel was set off from Egypt, so the universe

Satan from hence now on the lower stair   540
That scaled by steps of gold to heaven gate
Looks down with wonder at the sudden view
Of all this world at once. As when a scout
Through dark and desert ways with peril gone
All night; at last by break of cheerful dawn   545
Obtains the brow of some high-climbing hill,
Which to his eye discovers unaware
The goodly prospect of some foreign land
First-seen, or some renowned metropolis
With glistering spires and pinnacles adorned,   550
Which now the rising sun gilds with his beams.
Such wonder seized, though after heaven seen,
The spirit malign, but much more envy seized,
At sight of all this world beheld so fair.
Round he surveys, and well might, where he stood   555
So high above the circling canopy
Of night's extended shade; from eastern point
Of Libra to the fleecy star that bears
Andromeda far off Atlantic seas
Beyond the horizon; then from pole to pole   560
He views in breadth, and without longer pause
Down right into the world's first region throws

from Chaos; God **bound the ocean wave** at the parting of the Red Sea
(cf I 304–11) and M often links Pharaoh with Satan.   **543** Notice effect
of **all**. A **scout** goes on ahead of an army and his purpose is to betray the
place he seeks. (Structure: 'as when…who has gone'.)   **546 Obtains**
reaches. **high-climbing** could mean the hill or the scout, but either would
be appropriate to Satan's position on the golden stairs.   **552 after
heaven seen** though he had already seen heaven, the universe was no
anticlimax. He still feels this in IX 99: 'O earth, how like to heaven, if not
preferred More justly'.   **553 envy** whereas *wonder*, in the previous line,
identifies us with Satan's point of view, this detaches us. M uses similar
effects throughout.   **556 circling canopy** shadow of earth on the sky.
Normally above and circular; hence image; but directions are reversed
here.   **558 Libra** constellation of the scales (they play a crucial role at
end of IV). **fleecy star** Aries (the ram), which is next to **Andromeda**.
Try to picture this perspective on the universe, bearing in mind that the
zodiac would have run exactly parallel to the equator, not at an angle as
now. M describes the shift at X 668–77.   **562 first region** what we call
the ionosphere. It was thought (rightly) that mortals couldn't breathe
there. Notice effect of *throws* at end of line (and compare the much more

His flight precipitant, and winds with ease
Through the pure marble air his óblique way
Amongst innumerable stars, that shone   565
Stars distant, but nigh hand seemed other worlds,
Or other worlds they seemed, or happy isles,
Like those Hespérian gardens famed of old,
Fortunate fields, and groves and flowery vales,
Thrice happy isles, but who dwelt happy there   570
He stayed not to inquire: above them all
The golden sun in splendour likest heaven
Allured his eye: thither his course he bends
Through the calm firmament; but up or down
By centre, or eccentric, hard to tell,   575
Or longitude, where the great luminary
Aloof the vulgar constellations thick,
That from his lordly eye keep distance due,
Dispenses light from far; they as they move
Their starry dance in numbers that compute   580
Days, months, and years, towards his all-cheering lamp

cautious pause and take-off into Chaos II 917–29).   **563 winds** the rest
of Satan's flight is described as full of twists and turns (exuberant? sym-
bolic of deceit?); they're repeated in the sinuous rhythm of the lines.
564 marble air cold? unchanging? shining? Cf *Othello* III iii: 'Now by
yon marble heaven...'.   **566 distant** at a distance.   **568 Hespérian**
first of many images of mythical gardens (see IV 268–85 for others) asso-
ciated with earthly paradises. The golden apples of Jupiter were supposed
to grow in an island beyond the western seas; one of Hercules' labours
was to steal them.   **570 Thrice happy** because, if they were inhabited,
they escaped Satan's visit and the fall from innocence.   **571 above** in
which sense?   **573 bends** both 'directs' and 'swerves'.   **575 centre,
or eccentric** orbiting the centre of the universe (whether earth or sun) or
a point off-centre. Astronomical terms based on the medieval view of the
universe as a series of concentric spheres; when it was impossible to re-
concile the observed motion of a planet with this theory, astronomers as-
sumed that the centre of its orbit had been displaced. **hard to tell** because
M is not committing himself to a particular cosmology. Tone is humorous.
576 luminary the sun. The image of this 'lordly' spectator watching the
cosmic dance from a distance recalls the court masques of M's youth (and
Comus), where the dances were performed for the benefit of the
highest-ranking spectator.   **577 Aloof** at some distance from – but
M may intend the slightly off-putting effect, which distinguishes the
godlike sun from God himself.   **580 numbers** pun: rhythms of the
dance; also arithmetical computation which allows men to keep calendars
etc.

Turn swift their various motions, or are turned
By his magnetic beam, that gently warms
The universe, and to each inward part
With gentle penetration, though unseen,   585
Shoots invisible virtue even to the deep:
So wondrously was set his station bright.
There lands the fiend, a spot like which perhaps
Astronomer in the sun's lucent orb
Through his glazed optic tube yet never saw.   590

The place he found beyond expression bright,
Compared with aught on earth, metal or stone:
Not all parts like, but all alike informed
With radiant light, as glowing iron with fire;
If metal, part seemed gold, part silver clear;   595
If stone, carbuncle most or chrysolite,
Ruby or topaz, to the twelve that shone
In Aaron's breastplate, and a stone besides
Imagined rather oft than elsewhere seen,
That stone, or like to that which here below   600

582 Turn...or are turned leaves the question open; the magnetic theory
was first suggested by William Gilbert in 1600, then by Kepler in 1609.
586 Shoots stress this word. The rhythmic effects all through here are
worth noting: first the dance-like sound of 580–4, then the contrast be-
tween 'gentle' (twice) and the force of this line. The image is not only one
of violence; it also implies growth (shoots of grass etc). **virtue** influence;
comes from *vir* = man, which fits with the emphasis on the sun's mascu-
linity. **deep** the depths of either earth or sea (both thought of as feminine).
M is using traditional sexual imagery to explain the origin of gold and
precious stones by the action of the sun on buried materials.   **588–90** 'I
bet no astronomer ever saw a sunspot quite like *this* one': partly a joke and
partly implies doubt as to the existence of sunspots, over which there had
been much controversy since Galileo published his *Letters* on them in
1613. **optic tube** a normal 17c phrase; *telescope* didn't become standard
until late in the century.   **593–4** May be an analogy with heaven, where
all receive the light of God but in different degrees depending on their
capacities.   **598 Aaron's breastplate** described *Exodus* xxviii; it was
multicoloured embroidery covered with 12 different precious stones sym-
bolizing the 12 tribes of Israel (see Herbert's poem *Aaron*, which treats it
as symbolic of the virtues a true priest ought to have). **stone besides** the
philosopher's stone, sought by alchemists, which was supposed to turn
base metals to gold and give the possessor long life. Symbolic of Christ
(see Herbert's *Elixir*).

Philosophers in vain so long have sought,
In vain, though by their powerful art they bind
Volátile Hermes, and call up unbound
In various shapes old Proteus from the sea,
Drained through a limbeck to his native form.   605
What wonder then if fields and regions here
Breathe forth elixir pure, and rivers run
Potable gold, when with one virtuous touch
The arch-chemic sun so far from us remote
Produces with terrestrial humour mixed   610
Here in the dark so many precious things
Of colour glorious and effect so rare?
Here matter new to gaze the devil met
Undazzled, far and wide his eye commands,
For sight no obstacle found here, nor shade,   615
But all sunshíne, as when his beams at noon
Culminate from the equator, as they now
Shot upward still direct, whence no way round
Shadow from body opaque can fall, and the air,
No where so clear, sharpened his visual ray   620

601 in vain harks back to paradise of fools. 603 Volátile
Hermes quicksilver = mercury = the 'slippery' Greek god, symbol
of deceit = Satan. Alchemists tried to extract its essence to use
as material for transmutation. 604 Proteus the old man of the sea,
who had to be held while he went through a series of metamorphoses in
an effort to get loose (as in *Odyssey* IV) = matter without form = again,
an allusion to Satan's 'protean' disguises. 605 limbeck a container
with a long narrow neck, used for distillation. 607 elixir the 'stone'
in its liquid form. 608 Potable liquid – though gold was also drunk as
a cure at this period. virtuous both the modern sense and 'influential'.
609 arch-chemic master alchemist. Chemistry = transformation, and
alchemist is simply chemist prefixed by the Arabic definite article. 610
humour moisture (same root as humid); precious stones were thought to
be dew drops hardened in the sun. 612 effect medical. 613 matter
new something new, or newly transformed, to gaze (at). 614 Un-
dazzled Possible analogy with heaven? The sun, dazzling to look *at*, is
itself the source of clarity. Visualize: effect of light coming from below
rather than above; no shadows; a brightness that doesn't blind; perpetual
noon, but in reverse. 616 all sunshíne the stress helps one to hear the
full force of the meaning. 617 Culminate fall from the highest point of
the orbit, the celestial (not earthly) equator. 619 Scan: 'Shádow from
bódy opáque can fáll, and the áir'. The extra syllable adds lightness.
620 visual ray vision was thought to be a combination of rays from the

To objects distant far, whereby he soon
Saw within ken a glorious angel stand,
The same whom John saw also in the sun:
His back was turned, but not his brightness hid;
Of beaming sunny rays, a golden tiar   625
Circled his head, nor less his locks behind
Illustrious on his shoulders fledge with wings
Lay waving round; on some great charge employed
He seemed, or fixed in cogitation deep.

Glad was the spirit impure as now in hope   630
To find who might direct his wandering flight
To paradise the happy seat of man,
His journey's end and our beginning woe.
But first he casts to change his proper shape,
Which else might work him danger or delay: 635
And now a stripling cherub he appears,
Not of the prime, yet such as in his face
Youth smiled celestial, and to every limb
Suitable grace diffused, so well he feigned;
Under a coronet his flowing hair   640
In curls on either cheek played, wings he wore
Of many a coloured plume sprinkled with gold,

eye, the sun, and the object seen. Hence 'sharp' or 'piercing' eye (glances
like arrows). **622 ken** range within which one could know (ken) what
one saw. **glorious** in the state of glory (= sharing in the light of
God). **623 John** author of *Rev.*, where the angel is described as
prophesying the battle of Armageddon and the final binding of Satan in
the abyss (xix 17). **625 tiar** crown = a halo. **626–7 nor less** ie his
hair was no less **illustrious** (shining) than the halo (cf 361 above, where
hair and halo are similarly imagined). **fledge** feathered. **633 end** and
beginning emphasize the pattern here and in the poem; our **woe** will be
a **journey** like Satan's. **634 casts** schemes – with pun on other mean-
ings, such as casting a play or casting liquid metal. **proper** his own – but
of course it's proper for an evil spirit to look evil. **shape** could also mean
theatrical costume. **636 stripling cherub** angels are ageless but often
pictured as children. **637 prime** (of life). **639 grace** pun? **641
curls** though angels in pictures generally have curly hair, the general
effect of this description of the disguised Satan is too good to be true:
'Youth smiled…curls played…decent steps'.

His habit fit for speed succinct, and held
Before his decent steps a silver wand.
He drew not nigh unheard, the angel bright,   645
Ere he drew nigh, his radiant visage turned,
Admonished by his ear, and straight was known
The archangel Uriel, one of the seven
Who in God's presence, nearest to his throne
Stand ready at command, and are his eyes   650
That run through all the heavens, or down to the earth
Bear his swift errands over moist and dry,
O'er sea and land: him Satan thus accosts.
   'Uriel, for thou of those seven spirits that stand
In sight of God's high throne, gloriously bright,   655
The first art wont his great authentic will
Interpreter through highest heaven to bring,
Where all his sons thy embassy attend;
And here art likeliest by supreme decree
Like honour to obtain, and as his eye   660
To visit oft this new creation round;
Unspeakable desire to see, and know
All these his wondrous works, but chiefly man,
His chief delight and favour, him for whom
All these his works so wondrous he ordained,   665
Hath brought me from the choirs of cherubim
Alone thus wandering. Brightest seraph tell

---

643 succinct angels in flight are normally shown with long robes that conceal their feet; on the ground, they are tied up so that they blouse out below the waist. **644 decent** modest, respectful. **647 Admonished** warned. **648–52 Uriel** not a biblical name (except in the Apocryphal *Book of Esdras*) but the seven chief angels are in *Revelation* xx, where they are said to be symbolized by the seven stars in God's right hand, and the 'eyes of the Lord' in *Zechariah* iv. **657 Interpreter** as interpreter. **658 his sons** the angels. **660–1 as his eye** Satan suggests that Uriel may be stationed permanently on the sun, eye of the world, as a good place from which to observe all round the creation. See Donne's *Sun rising*. **662 Unspeakable** inexpressible. **664 favour** favourite. **666–7 cherubim** angels primarily dedicated to divine knowledge (in art, often painted blue). **seraphim** highest order, dedicated to love, often painted red. But protestants were sceptical of elaborate categories of angels, and M uses these terms more or less interchangeably.

In which of all these shining orbs hath man
His fixèd seat, or fixèd seat hath none,
But all these shining orbs his choice to dwell;   670
That I may find him, and with secret gaze,
Or open admiration him behold
On whom the great creator hath bestowed
Worlds, and on whom hath all these graces poured;
That both in him and all things, as is meet,   675
The universal maker we may praise;
Who justly hath driven out his rebel foes
To deepest hell, and to repair that loss
Created this new happy race of men
To serve him better: wise are all his ways.'   680

So spake the false dissembler unperceived;
For neither man nor angel can discern
Hypocrisy, the only evil that walks
Invisible, except to God alone,
By his permissive will, through heaven and earth: 685
And oft though wisdom wake, suspicion sleeps
At wisdom's gate, and to simplicity
Resigns her charge, while goodness thinks no ill
Where no ill seems: which now for once beguiled
Uriel, though regent of the sun, and held   690
The sharpest sighted spirit of all in heaven;
Who to the fraudulent imposter foul
In his uprightness answer thus returned.

668–70 Reminds us that Satan doesn't know who or where man is, though he may be exaggerating his naivety for Uriel's benefit. **675 meet** fitting. **680 To serve him better** perhaps hidden sarcasm, in view of Satan's view of God as a tyrant? The whole speech is very formally structured; notice also the neat conclusion, **ways** rhyming with *praise* (676). **681 unperceived** undetected. **685 permissive will** theological distinction: God does not approve of hypocrisy, but by permitting it to exist he in a sense wills it. **687 wisdom's gate** a suitable metaphor: Satan has already passed through the gate to the universe and Uriel is about to let him into its inner sanctum. **689 which** hypocrisy – notice effect of long parenthesis. **690 regent** a temporary substitute for the rightful ruler (ie God), also mover and guide.

'Fair angel, thy desire which tends to know
The works of God, thereby to glorify   695
The great work-master, leads to no excess
That reaches blame, but rather merits praise
The more it seems excess, that led thee hither
From thy empýreal mansion thus alone,
To witness with thine eyes what some perhaps   700
Contented with report hear only in heaven:
For wonderful indeed are all his works,
Pleasant to know, and worthiest to be all
Had in remembrance always with delight;
But what created mind can comprehend   705
Their number, or the wisdom infinite
That brought them forth, but hid their causes deep?
I saw when at his word the formless mass,
This world's material mould, came to a heap:
Confusion heard his voice, and wild uproar   710
Stood ruled, stood vast infinitude confined;
Till at his second bidding darkness fled,
Light shone, and order from disorder sprung:
Swift to their several quarters hasted then
The cumbrous elements, earth, flood, air, fire,   715
And this ethereal quíntessénce of heaven
Flew upward, spirited with various forms,
That rolled orbicular, and turned to stars
Numberless, as thou seest, and how they move;
Each had his place appointed, each his course,   720
The rest in circuit walls this universe.
Look downward on that globe whose hither side

694 **tends** is directed to.   699 **mansion** biblical (NEB translates as
room): dwelling.   701 **hear only** only *hear*.   705 **comprehend** both
understand and compass.   707 **deep** goes with both *causes* and *hid*.
709 **material mould** Chaos, the unformed matter from which the
universe was made. **came to a heap** !   710 **Confusion** a personification
(the same may be true of **uproar** etc); see II 959–67 for the followers of
Chaos.   716 **quíntessénce** the fifth element, ether, the substance of
everything above the moon's sphere.   717 **spirited** a platonic des-
cription of lifeless matter (Chaos) receiving soul and form.   718
orbicular circular.   721 **in circuit** in an outer sphere.

76

With light from hence, though but reflected, shines;
That place is earth the seat of man, that light
His day, which else as the other hemisphere   725
Night would invade, but there the neighbouring moon
(So call that opposite fair star) her aid
Timely interposes, and her monthly round
Still ending, still renewing, through mid heaven;
With borrowed light her countenance triform   730
Hence fills and empties to enlighten the earth,
And in her pale dominion checks the night.
That spot to which I point is paradise,
Adam's abode, those lofty shades his bower.
Thy way thou canst not miss, me mine requires.'   735
    Thus said, he turned, and Satan bowing low,
As to superior spirits is wont in heaven,
Where honour due and reverence none neglects,
Took leave, and toward the coast of earth beneath,
Down from the ecliptic, sped with hoped success,   740
Throws his steep flight in many an airy wheel,
Nor stayed, till on Niphátès' top he lights.

726 Night would invade ironically refers to Satan's own project. **there** in
the other hemisphere (stress it in reading).   **727 her aid** the moon is
usually feminine and her relation to the sun is a traditional symbol for
woman in her ideal relation to man.   **728 Timely** both in time and regu-
larly. Moon continues to be the subject all through this long and complica-
ted sentence.   **730 triform** because there were three phases during which
the moon was visible: full, half, and quarter.   **731 Hence** from the sun.
fills and empties goes better with the image of urns at a fountain in VII
359–66 than with the moon's personified *countenance*.   **733–4** As often,
the view, even from a great distance, is amazingly clear, though in this case
the clarity may be due to the special conditions on the sun.   **735 me
mine requires** stress both *me* and *mine*.   **737 wont** customary.   **739
coast** side.   **740 ecliptic** the sun's apparent orbit (or, we should now
say, the earth's orbit), passing through the signs of the zodiac. **with hoped
success** both with hope of success and with the success (result) he had
hoped for.   **741 an airy wheel** since Eden is directly under him, this
curving motion is unnecessary; perhaps it foreshadows his serpent role.
742 Niphátès a mountain in Assyria, within sight of the traditional loca-
tion of Eden, Mesopotamia. One of the rivers of paradise, the Tigris,
originates here, so Satan's position on earth corresponds to his position
on the foot of the heavenly stair. It's an appropriate place for his soliloquy
in IV.

Book IV

O FOR THAT WARNING VOICE, which he who saw
The apocalypse, heard cry in heaven aloud,
Then when the dragon, put to second rout,
Came furious down to be revenged on men,
'Woe to the inhabitants on earth!' that now,   5
While time was, our first parents had been warned
The coming of their secret foe, and scaped,
Haply so scaped his mortal snare; for now
Satan, now first inflamed with rage, came down,
The tempter ere the accuser of mankind,   10
To wreak on innocent frail man his loss
Of that first battle, and his flight to hell;
Yet not rejoicing in his speed, though bold,
Far off and fearless, nor with cause to boast,
Begins his dire attempt, which nigh the birth   15
Now rolling, boils in his tumultuous breast,
And like a devilish engine back recoils
Upon himself; horror and doubt distract
His troubled thoughts, and from the bottom stir
The hell within him, for within him hell   20
He brings, and round about him, nor from hell
One step no more than from himself can fly
By change of place: now conscience wakes despair
That slumbered, wakes the bitter memory
Of what he was, what is, and what must be   25
Worse; of worse deeds worse sufferings must ensue.
Sometimes towards Eden which now in his view

---

2 **apocalypse** *Revelation* xii: 'Woe to the inhabitants of the earth...for
the devil is come down unto you'. All the invocations have to do with
voices or hearing.   8 **scaped** escaped; cf repeated *now*, and line 20.
26 **Worse** crashing stress.   27 **Eden** the word meant pleasure.

78

Lay pleasant, his grieved look he fixes sad,
Sometimes towards heaven and the full-blazing sun,
Which now sat high in his meridian tower: 30
Then much revolving, thus in sighs began.

  'O thou that with surpassing glory crowned,
Look'st from thy sole dominion like the God
Of this new world; at whose sight all the stars
Hide their diminished heads; to thee I call,   35
But with no friendly voice, and add thy name
O sun, to tell thee how I hate thy beams
That bring to my remembrance from what state
I fell, how glorious once above thy sphere;
Till pride and worse ambition threw me down   40
Warring in heaven against heaven's matchless
    king:
Ah wherefore! He deserved no such return
From me, whom he created what I was
In that bright eminence, and with his good
Upbraided none; nor was his service hard.   45
What could be less than to afford him praise,
The easiest recompense, and pay him thanks,
How due! Yet all his good proved ill in me,
And wrought but malice; lifted up so high
I sdeigned subjection, and thought one step   50
    higher
Would set me highest, and in a moment quit
The debt immense of endless gratitude,
So burdensome still paying, still to owe;
Forgetful what from him I still received,
And understood not that a grateful mind   55
By owing owes not, but still pays, at once
Indebted and discharged; what burden then?
O had his powerful destiny ordained
Me some inferior angel, I had stood

30 meridian tower noon verticality.   **31 revolving** pondering.   **48**
ill evil.   **50 sdeigned** disdained. **subjection** subordination.

Then happy; no unbounded hope had raised   60
Ambition. Yet why not? Some other power
As great might have aspired, and me though mean
Drawn to his part; but other powers as great
Fell not, but stand unshaken, from within
Or from without, to all temptations armed.   65
Hadst thou the same free will and power to stand?
Thou hadst: whom hast thou then or what to accuse,
But heaven's free love dealt equally to all?
Be then his love accursed, since love or hate,
To me alike, it deals eternal woe.   70
Nay cursed be thou; since against his thy will
Chose freely what it now so justly rues.

    Me miserable! Which way shall I fly
Infinite wrath, and infinite despair?
Which way I fly is hell; my self am hell;   75
And in the lowest deep a lower deep
Still threatening to devour me opens wide,
To which the hell I suffer seems a heaven.

    O then at last relent: is there no place
Left for repentance, none for pardon left?   80
None left but by submission; and that word
Disdain forbids me, and my dread of shame
Among the spirits beneath, whom I seduced
With other promises and other vaunts
Than to submit, boasting I could subdue   85
The omnipotent. Ay me, they little know
How dearly I abide that boast so vain,
Under what torments inwardly I groan;
While they adore me on the throne of hell,
With diadem and sceptre high advanced   90
The lower still I fall, only supreme
In misery; such joy ambition finds.
But say I could repent and could obtain

60 unbounded...Ambition motives of renaissance tragic heroes.   **62 mean** unimportant. Even had he been a lower angel (power), he might have followed another high rebel.   **66 free will** for this and the imagery of stand–fall see III 102.   **75 Which** whichever.

By act of grace my former state; how soon
Would highth recall high thoughts, how soon unsay   95
What feigned submission swore; ease would recant
Vows made in pain, as violent and void.
For never can true reconcilement grow
Where wounds of deadly hate have pierced so deep:
Which would but lead me to a worse relapse   100
And heavier fall: so should I purchase dear
Short intermission bought with double smart.
This knows my punisher; therefore as far
From granting he, as I from begging peace:
All hope excluded thus, behold in stead   105
Of us outcást, exíled, his new delight,
Mankind created, and for him this world.
    So farewell hope, and with hope farewell fear,
Farewell remorse: all good to me is lost;
Evil be thou my good; by thee at least   110
Divided empire with heaven's king I hold
By thee, and more than half perhaps will reign;
As man ere long, and this new world shall know.'
    Thus while he spake, each passion dimmed his face
Thrice changed with pale, ire, envy and despair,   115
Which marred his borrowed visage, and betrayed
Him counterfeit, if any eye beheld.
For heavenly minds from such distempers foul
Are ever clear. Whereof he soon aware,
Each perturbation smoothed with outward calm,   120
Artíficer of fraud; and was the first
That practised falsehood under saintly show,
Deep malice to conceal, couched with revenge:
Yet not enough had practised to deceive
Uriel once warned; whose eye pursued him down   125
The way he went, and on the Assyrian mount

110 **Evil** still theatrical; cf Shakespeare's *Richard III*. This speech was
probably the first part of *PL* M wrote, as for a tragedy.   114 **passion**
emotion, each supposed to have its own complexion. A cherub (which he
is disguised as) should be red of face; he turns thrice pale.   125 **Uriel**
III 622.   126 **Assyrian** Mt Niphates III 742.

Saw him disfigured, more than could befall
Spirit of happy sort: his gestures fierce
He marked and mad demeanour, then alone,
As he supposed, all unobserved, unseen.   130

So on he fares, and to the border comes,
Of Eden, where delicious paradise,
Now nearer, crowns with her enclosure green,
As with a rural mound the champaign head
Of a steep wilderness, whose hairy sides   135
With thicket overgrown, grotesque and wild,
Access denied; and over head up grew
Insuperable highth of loftiest shade,
Cedar, and pine, and fir, and branching palm,
A sylvan scene, and as the ranks ascend   140
Shade above shade, a woody theätre
Of stateliest view. Yet higher than their tops
The verdurous wall of paradise up sprung:
Which to our general sire gave prospect large
Into his nether empire neighbouring round.   145
And higher than that wall a circling row
Of goodliest trees loaden with fairest fruit,
Blossoms and fruits at once of golden hue
Appeared, with gay enamelled colours mixed:
On which the sun more glad impressed his beams   150
Than in fair evening cloud, or humid bow,

131 border first of series of boundary words here.   **134 champaign** open country. M is thinking of something like the clumps of trees that grow on prehistoric earthworks on top of bare level downs, eg Chanctonbury Ring in Sussex, Wandlebury just outside Cambridge. Also of pudendum.   **136 grotesque** romantic, interwoven foliage.   **137 denied** the sides stopped anyone getting in. In the next lines it is as if Satan then looked up and up to find a way.   **138 shade** often used in 17c to mean trees.   **139 palm** seems out of place with conifers but biblical and Mediterranean.   **140 sylvan** quoted in *Waste land* where Eliot describes a rich sterile boudoir; and by Hopkins in *Binsey poplars*.   **143 verdurous** made of green vegetation, like a grassy earthwork.   **144 general sire** father of the species, Adam. **prospect** a view.   **148 at once** instead of consecutively – perpetual spring–summer.   **149 enamelled** lustrous.   **151 bow** the fruit shine more

When God hath showered the earth; so lovely seemed
That landscape. And of pure now purer air
Meets his approach, and to the heart inspires
Vernal delight and joy, able to drive   155
All sadness but despair: now gentle gales
Fanning their odoriferous wings dispense
Native perfúmes, and whisper whence they stole
Those balmy spoils. As when to them who sail
Beyond the Cape of Hope, and now are past   160
Mozámbic, off at sea north-east winds blow
Sabéän odours from the spicy shore
Of Arabie the blest, with such delay
Well pleased they slack their course, and many a league
Cheered with the grateful smell old Ocean smiles.   165
So entertained those odorous sweets the fiend
Who came their bane, though with them better pleased
Than Asmodeüs with the fishy fume,
That drove him, though enamoured, from the spouse

brightly than sunset and rainbow; land lovelier than sky.   **153 of** from.
Change from colours to smells.   **156 gales** winds (not storms).   **158
Native** they belong to paradise, instead of being brought as costly mer-
chandise (spoils) from the east; but I don't understand why the winds
whisper where they come from; or does the wind sound like the word
paradise?   **160 Hope** Good Hope. First rounded for India by da Gama
1486. See R. R. Cawley *M and the literature of travel* and consider the
Cape's place in the imagination, and in commerce, before Suez Canal.
See a map: the ships are sailing NE into the Indian Ocean, against head-
winds. Sabean refers to Sheba, now Yemen. Arabia *felix* was the fertile
part as opposed to *deserta*. Milton had read Diodorus Siculus, a Greek
historian writing just before Christ of this region: 'When the wind is
blowing offshore, one finds that the sweet odours exhaled by the myrrh-
bearing and other aromatic trees penetrate to the nearby parts of the sea.'
165 grateful pleasing. The smell calms the sea.   **166 entertained** re-
ceived. Note how 1½ lines switch one simile into another.   **168 Asmo-
deüs** even though he enjoyed the smell, Satan was in the same class as the
evil spirit Asmodeus: he killed seven husbands of a girl called Rachel, in
Media, one after the other, before they could get into bed with her. The
eighth, Tobias the son of Tobit, asked help of the angel Raphael; Raphael
advised him to burn the heart and liver of a fish. The stench of the smoke
(fume) drove Asmodeus to Egypt, where Raphael tied him up. (*Tobit* is a
book in the OT Apocrypha.) Devils often exorcised by sweet smoke
(incense), and often emit stink (Satan appeared to Luther in the privy).
Asmodeus recurs VI 365; he is 'the fleshliest incubus' *PR* II 151. Simile
shifts sweet to rotten, rural to sexual; shocking?

Of Tobit's son, and with a vengeance sent   170
From Media post to Aegypt, there fast bound.

  Now to the ascent of that steep savage hill
Satan had journeyed on, pensive and slow;
But further way found none, so thick entwined,
As one continued brake, the undergrowth   175
Of shrubs and tangling bushes had perplexed
All path of man or beast that passed that way:
One gate there only was, and that looked east
On the other side: which when the arch-felon saw
Due entrance he disdained, and in contempt,   180
At one slight bound high over leaped all bound
Of hill or highest wall, and sheer within
Lights on his feet. As when a prowling wolf,
Whom hunger drives to seek new haunt for prey,
Watching where shepherds pen their flocks at eve   185
In hurdled cotes amid the field secure,
Leaps o'er the fence with ease into the fold:
Or as a thief bent to unhoard the cash
Of some rich burgher, whose substantial doors,
Cross-barred and bolted fast, fear no assault,   190
In at the window climbs, or o'er the tiles;
So clomb this first grand thief into God's fold:
So since into his church lewd hirelings climb.
Thence up he flew, and on the tree of life,
The middle tree and highest there that grew,   195
Sat like a cormorant; yet not true life
Thereby regained, but sat devising death

175 brake thicket.　　**176 perplexed** would have tangled.　　**181 bound**
he bounds over the boundary, oversteps the limit, transgresses.　　**184
haunt** hunting-ground. Cf vulture III 431. For Jesus as the good shep-
herd who defends against the wolf, and others as the hireling, see *John*
x, and *Lyc* 115: line 193 is in M's own voice and time.　　**193 lewd** vile;
or ignorant. Many clergy were uneducated; many were in the church for
profit rather than religion.　　**196 cormorant** emblem of gaping greed.
Satan seems to have turned into one – he often metamorphoses. The tree
of life was regarded as a symbol of immortality; the tree of knowledge as
a symbol of obedience.

To them who lived; nor on the virtue thought
Of that life-giving plant, but only used
For prospect, what well used had been the pledge   200
Of immortality. So little knows
Any, but God alone, to value right
The good before him, but perverts best things
To worst abuse, or to their meanest use.

Beneath him with new wonder now he views   205
To all delight of human sense exposed
In narrow room nature's whole wealth, yea more,
A heaven on earth, for blissful paradise
Of God the garden was, by him in the east
Of Eden planted; Eden stretched her line   210
From Auran eastward to the royal towers
Of great Seleucia, built by Grecian kings,
Or where the sons of Eden long before
Dwelt in Telassar: in this pleasant soil
His far more pleasant garden God ordained;   215
Out of the fertile ground he caused to grow
All trees of noblest kind for sight, smell, taste;
And all amid them stood the tree of life,
High eminent, blooming ambrosial fruit   *effective use of*
Of vegetable gold; and next to life   *caesura*   220
Our death the tree of knowledge grew fast by,   *& enjambement*
Knowledge of good bought dear by knowing ill.
   Southward through Eden went a river large,

206 Emphatic rhythms, 'all' words, eg 'whóle wéalth'   **210 line**
frontiers. Paradise was still sought by 17c explorers; it was thought
to lie either between the sources of Tigris and Euphrates or at their
confluence. See *Gen.* ii. Seleucia near Bagdad, on Tigris, was built
by one of Alexander's generals – the allusion asserts the fall; so do
Telassar, and Haran (near Damascus) – cited in *II Kings* xix as places
which have been destroyed, their kings no more.   **219 ambrosial**
delicious and immortalizing like drink of the gods.   **220 vegetable gold**
golden fruit, nature + art; and metal that is alive and growing; and a
variety of the alchemical 'philosopher's stone' or elixir of life.   **223**
Southward abrupt return to larger geography; is the whole description
ordered or chaotic? Satan uses the Tigris to get back into paradise IX 70.
The osmotic watering dispenses with rain.

Nor changed his course, but through the shaggy hill
Passed underneath ingulfed, for God had thrown   225
That mountain as his garden mould high raised
Upon the rapid current, which through veins
Of porous earth with kindly thirst up drawn,
Rose a fresh fountain, and with many a rill
Watered the garden; thence united fell   230
Down the steep glade, and met the nether flood,
Which from his darksome passage now appears,
And now divided into four main streams,
Runs diverse, wandering many a famous realm
And country whereof here needs no account,   235
But rather to tell how, if art could tell,
How from that sapphire fount the crispèd brooks,
Rolling on orient pearl and sands of gold,
With mazy error under pendant shades
Ran nectar, visiting each plant, and fed   240
Flowers worthy of paradise which not nice art
In beds and curious knots, but nature boon
Poured forth profuse on hill and dale and plain,
Both where the morning sun first warmly smote
The open field, and where the unpierced shade   245
Embrowned the noontide bowers: thus was this place,
A happy rural seat of various view;
Groves whose rich trees wept odorous gums and balm,
Others whose fruit burnished with golden rind
Hung amiable, Hesperian fables true,   250

234 **wandering** loose vague lines here; syntax dissolves at 236.   **237
crispèd** waved like hair.   **238 orient** lustrous. The jewels come from
Gen. ii, *Ezekiel* xxviii; they were also used by explorers to describe places
in America and Africa.   **239 mazy error** meandering; both words toll
through the poem eg VII 20, 50, 302; IX 499, 1049, 1136, 1146; X 830,
875, 969; XII 648.   **241 nice** exquisite. The contrast is with 16–17c
flowerbeds shaped like true-love-knots or mazes. With 'nature boon'
another passage of astounding potency starts its rhythms.   **246 Em-
browned** darkened; Italian *imbrunire* = to shade. 17c painters used
brown for shade, as early 20c painters used violet. Complex local
pattern open/closed, morning/noon, with continuing suggestion of human
bodies and copulation since 137.   **247 seat** the whole line is of the sort
used in the 17c to describe a country house and its park.   **250 amiable**

86

If true, here only, and of delicious taste:
Betwixt them lawns, or level downs, and flocks
Grazing the tender herb, were interposed,
Or palmy hillock, or the flowery lap
Of some irriguous valley spread her store,   255
Flowers of all hue, and without thorn the rose:
Another side, umbrageous grots and caves
Of cool recess, o'er which the mantling vine
Lays forth her purple grape, and gently creeps
Luxuriant; mean while murmuring waters fall   260
Down the slope hills, dispersed, or in a lake,
That to the fringèd bank with myrtle crowned,
Her crystal mirror holds, unite their streams.
The birds their choir apply; airs, vernal airs,
Breathing the smell of field and grove, attune   265
The trembling leaves, while universal Pan
Knit with the Graces and the Hours in dance
Led on the eternal spring.

                      Not that fair field
Of Enna, where Prosérpine gathering flowers

lovely. Syntax drifts off again – if the stories of the Hesperian gardens of
the west (see *evening* in Greek and Latin), where a tree of golden apples
was guarded by a dragon and maidens, were true, then they would be
true only here. See Burne-Jones' picture. Taste warns of the fall, which is
used as a verb in 260; cf I 2, V and IX passim.   **252 Betwixt** between
the groves. Lawns were glades. Seems chaotic again.   **255 irriguous**
well watered. Consider lap.   **263 mirror** I find this sentence confusing.
264 apply supply. Airs = tune and wind; music = scent; cf Baudelaire's
'hautbois verts comme les prairies'.   **266 Pan** the allegory means that
all natural things, joined with sexuality and the seasons, ensured perpetual
springtime. Pan (= all) was god of nature. The Graces were the three girls,
always shown linked in a dance to balance their qualities, Chastity or
Youth, Beauty or Maturity, and Love or Desire. The Hours (Horae) were the
three goddesses who represented the ordered sequence of the seasons; they
all smelled of spring. The best way to study this passage is to look at Botti-
celli's painting *Primavera* and commentary on it in Wind *Pagan mysteries
in the renaissance*; see also Poussin's *Dance to the music of time* in *JM :
introductions* in this series.   **268 Not** note negative structure to multiple
simile as if pushing away the world every time it is invoked, then sliding
back into paradise at 285.   **269 Enna** Persephone, daughter of Zeus

Her self a fairer flower by gloomy Dis   270
Was gathered, which cost Cerës all that pain
To seek her through the world; nor that sweet grove
Of Daphne by Orontes, and the inspired
Castalian spring, might with this paradise
Of Eden strive; nor that Nyseian isle   275
Girt with the river Triton, where old Cham,
Whom Gentiles Ammon call and Lybian Jove,
Hid Amalthea and her florid son
Young Bacchus from his stepdame Rhea's eye;
Nor where Abássin kings their issue guard,   280
Mount Ámara, though this by some supposed
True paradise under the Ethiop line

(sky god) and Ceres (or Demeter, earth, corn goddess), was gathering
flowers at Enna in Sicily when the earth opened and Dis (god of the under-
world, Hades, Pluto) on his black horses abducted her. Ceres made the
world barren by forbidding trees to yield while she sought her everywhere.
At last, with the help of animal herdsmen, she found the girl; but Perse-
phone had eaten seven pomegranate seeds, the food of the dead, in hades,
and as wife to Dis, become queen of the underworld; so she was able to
return to the upper world for only half the year; that is why it is bare of
crops for the other half. Christ the corn god suffered for Eve; she is a
flower again at IX 432, the temptation.   **273 Daphne** really refers to the
same place as 'the royal towers Of great Seleucia' at 211. It was the name
of a magnificent park on the river Orontes outside Antioch in Syria. There
was a grove of laurel and cypress 10 miles round, watered by natural
springs, which General Seleucus dedicated to Apollo. (Hence the water is
inspired, and named after the Castalian spring on Mt Parnassus.) A temple
was built there, with a splendid statue of Apollo. The legend of Daphne,
which belongs to Greece, was transferred here: when Apollo tried to rape
her she ran away, then turned into a laurel tree (*daphne*) in his hands; see
the sculpture by Bernini. Another site of drastic change.   **275 Nyseian**
one of a number of places called Nysa where Dionysus was supposed to
have been brought up. This one was in a lake just inland from the north
coast of Africa (now a dried salt lake near Tunis). King Ammon of Libya
(supposed also to be Noah's son Ham, and the African version of Jove)
impregnated Amalthea. She bore a wonderful baby, Dionysus (Bacchus).
To protect them both from the wrath of his wife Rhea (the child's step-
mother) he hid them on Nysa. Dionysus grew up to be the god of wine,
red-faced from drinking. I don't think anybody has ever suggested why
this simile winds itself into such spirals of detail.   **281 Ámara** range of
hills in Abyssinia; a contemporary traveller described a high shining sum-
mit with a palace on it where the king's sons were kept safe from sedition;
so beautiful 'that some have taken (but mistaken) it for the place of
paradise'. He also thought it was near the equator (Ethiop line).

By Nilus' head, enclosed with shining rock,
A whole day's journey high, but wide remote
From this Assyrian garden, where the fiend   285
Saw undelighted all delight, all kind
Of living creatures new to sight and strange:
Two of far nobler shape erect and tall,
Godlike erect, with native honour clad
In naked majesty seemed lords of all,   290
And worthy seemed, for in their looks divine
The image of their glorious maker shone,
Truth, wisdom, sanctitude severe and pure,
Severe but in true filial freedom placed;
Whence true authority in men; though both   295
Not equal, as their sex not equal seemed;
For contemplation he and valour formed,
For softness she and sweet attractive grace,
He for God only, she for God in him:
His fair large front and eye sublime declared   300
Absolute rule; and hyacinthine locks.
Round from his parted forelock manly hung
Clustering, but not beneath his shoulders broad:
She as a veil down to the slender waist

285 Assyrian he means in the strict sense of the eastern hinterland of the Tigris; invitation to consult map and *Gen.* ii; yet implies paradise no more to be found.   **289 native** what you're born with. Assonance with naked. Both phrases paradoxical.   **293 Truth...** these are qualities of God. It's difficult to be sure about 294: why are severity and freedom opposed? Probably severe means absolute, strictly conforming to the image of God; but nevertheless that image is here located (like a family likeness) in the freedom of man, God's child. It is from the image of God in man that true authority derives – rather, M thought, than from ancestry or office.   **296 equal** he shifts from 'not identical' to 'superior/inferior'; and the sexual analogy is clearly based on a man's perception; but M's case here was orthodox for the time.   **297 contemplation** thinking; at VIII 40 Eve leaves him to it. VIII 452–611 relates Adam's feelings about her.   **300 front** forehead. **sublime** prominent; cf heroic statues, and the significance of the eyes of actual leaders.   **301 hyacinthine** buoyantly curling, like Odysseus' hair when he was rescued from the sea and 'Athena lent a hand, making him seem | taller, and massive too, with crisping hair | in curls like petals of wild hyacinth, | but all red-golden. Think of gold infused | on silver by a craftsman...just so she lavished | beauty over Odysseus' head and shoulders' *Odyssey* VI 231. Adam is usually beardless, as here.   **304 veil**

Her unadornèd golden tresses wore   305
Dishevelled, but in wanton ringlets waved
As the vine curls her tendrils, which implied
Subjection, but required with gentle sway,
And by her yielded, by him best received,
Yielded with coy submission, modest pride,   310
And sweet reluctant amorous delay.
Nor those mysterious parts were then concealed,
Then was not guilty shame, dishonest shame
Of nature's works, honour dishonourable,
Sin-bred, how have ye troubled all mankind   315
With shows instead, mere shows of seeming
        pure,
And banished from man's life his happiest life,
Simplicity and spotless innocence.
So passed they naked on, nor shunned the sight
Of God or angel, for they thought no ill: 320
So hand in hand they passed, the loveliest pair
That ever since in love's embraces met,
Adam the goodliest man of men since born
His sons, the fairest of her daughters Eve.
Under a tuft of shade that on a green   325
Stood whispering soft, by a fresh fountain side
They sat them down, and after no more toil
Of their sweet gardening labour than sufficed
To recommend cool zephyr, and made ease
More easy, wholesome thirst and appetite   330
More grateful, to their supper fruits they fell,

not clear why she needs one in view of 313. See analysis of this pas-
sage in preface. Her longer hair both the glory of woman and sign of sub-
jection to husband (*I Corinthians* xi). The rules change; but the relations
between men and women in society always are marked by hair.   **310 coy**
quiet, reserved.   **312 mysterious** sacramental (Greek *mysterion* = re-
ligious rite); and secret. Cf Donne's lovers in *Canonization*: their coitus is
mysterious like death and resurrection. See 743.   **313 dishonest** impure
(honesty often = sexual faith).   **314 dishonourable** big stress on *dis-*.
Repeats form of previous line but sways without syntax out of the poem.
Taken up again 744.   **323–4** Note Adam…born…Eve structure.   **326
fountain** spring.   **331 fell**! Note the mouth words hereabouts.

Nectarine fruits which the compliant boughs
Yielded them, sidelong as they sat recline
On the soft downy bank damasked with flowers:
The savoury pulp they chew, and in the rind   335
Still as they thirsted scoop the brimming stream;
Nor gentle purpose, nor endearing smiles
Wanted, nor youthful dalliance as beseems
Fair couple, linked in happy nuptial league,
Alone as they. About them frisking played   340
All beasts of the earth, since wild, and of all chase
In wood or wilderness, forest or den;
Sporting the lion ramped, and in his paw
Dandled the kid; bears, tigers, ounces, pards,
Gambolled before them, the unwieldy elephant   345
To make them mirth used all his might, and wreathed
His lithe proboscis; close the serpent sly
Insinuating, wove with Gordian twine
His braided train, and of his fatal guile
Gave proof unheeded; others on the grass   350
Couched, and now filled with pasture gazing sat,
Or bedward ruminating: for the sun
Declined was hasting now with prone career
To the Ocean Isles, and in the ascending scale
Of heaven the stars that usher evening rose.   355

When Satan still in gaze, as first he stood,
Scarce thus at length failed speech recovered sad.

332 Nectarine ambrosial (219).   **334 downy** soft as down, like an em-
broidered pillow.   **337 gentle purpose** decent talk. This and dalliance
(love play) were not lacking.   **341 since wild** they become wild at x
710.   **344 ounces, pards** lynx, leopards.   **348 Gordian twine** coil
as hard to undo as the Gordian knot, which Alexander the Great cut. The
serpent reappears for the temptation IX 499; but really it is Satan in him
that is fatal.   **349 braided train** plaited length.   **352 ruminating**
chewing the cud before going to bed.   **354 Isles** Azores, as 592. **scale**
the poem poises with this balancing of light/dark. The evening star,
Venus, appears to rise opposite the sun. At the supposed season it would
seem to rise in the constellation Libra, Scales.   **357 Rhythm falters.**

'O hell! What do mine eyes with grief behold,
Into our room of bliss thus high advanced
Creatures of other mould, earth-born perhaps,   360
Not spirits, yet to heavenly spirits bright
Little inferior; whom my thoughts pursue
With wonder, and could love, so lively shines
In them divine resemblance, and such grace
The hand that formed them on their shape hath poured. 365
    Ah gentle pair, ye little think how nigh
Your change approaches, when all these delights
Will vanish and deliver ye to woe,
More woe, the more your taste is now of joy;
Happy, but for so happy ill secured   370
Long to continue, and this high seat your heaven
Ill fenced for heaven to keep out such a foe
As now is entered; yet no purposed foe
To you whom I could pity thus forlorn
Though I unpitied: league with you I seek,   375
And mutual amity so strait, so close,
That I with you must dwell, or you with me
Henceforth; my dwelling haply may not please
Like this fair paradise, your sense, yet such
Accept your maker's work; he gave it me,   380
Which I as freely give; hell shall unfold,
To entertain you two, her widest gates,
And send forth all her kings; there will be room,

359 room *Lebensraum.* **360 earth-born** if man did not come out of
the earth (autochthonous) where did he come from? And is the earth-born
inferior, is it necessarily unspiritual? Renaissance especially interested in
the paradox stated in *Psalm* viii and *Hebrews* ii: 'Thou hast made him a
little lower than the angels, and hast crowned him with glory and honour';
cf *Hamlet* II ii: 'What a piece of work is man...how like an angel...the
paragon of animals! And yet...this quintessence of dust.' **364** The
lines caress and sculpt. **366 gentle** noble. **370 secured** less safe
than happy. Rhetoric twists and returns on woe...happy...ill and several
other themes, and sounds. **372 for heaven** badly defended, as
heavens go. **375 league** political perversion of the love of 339. **377
with you...with me** syntax presents inner and outer hells, the evil in us,
and damnation. **380 Accept** you'll have to accept that God made hell
as well as paradise. Satan goes on to talk like Tamburlaine.

Not like these narrow limits, to receive
Your numerous offspring; if no better place,   385
Thank him who puts me loth to this revenge
On you who wrong me not for him who wronged.
And should I at your harmless innocence
Melt, as I do, yet public reason just,
Honour and empire with revenge enlarged   390
By conquering this new world, compels me now
To do what else though damned I should abhor.'
    So spake the fiend, and with necessity,
The tyrant's plea, excused his devilish deeds.

Then from his lofty stand on that high tree   395
Down he alights among the sportful herd
Of those four-footed kinds, himself now one,
Now other, as their shape served best his end
Nearer to view his prey, and unespied
To mark what of their state he more might learn   400
By word or action marked: about them round
A lion now he stalks with fiery glare,
Then as a tiger, who by chance hath spied
In some purlieu two gentle fawns at play,
Straight couches close, then rising changes oft   405
His couchant watch, as one who chose his ground
Whence rushing he might surest seize them both
Griped in each paw: when Adam first of men
To first of women Eve thus moving speech,
Turned him all ear to hear new utterance flow.   410
    'Sole partner and sole part of all these joys,
Dearer thy self than all; needs must the power
That made us, and for us this ample world

384 limits moral and physical boundaries of paradise.   **387 for him**
instead of him. Satan's revenge on man instead of God versus God's
justice on Christ instead of man.   **398 shape** parody of incarnation; re-
hearsal for fall when he enters the snake; theme of changefulness,
instability.   **410 ear** seems to mean that Adam's voice turns Satan into
an ear now – 'I'm all ears'; even that he enters Adam and Eve's ears?
413 for us *for* us stressed colloquially.

Be infinitely good, and of his good
As liberal and free as infinite,   415
That raised us from the dust and placed us here
In all this happiness, who at his hand
Have nothing merited, nor can perform
Aught whereof he hath need, he who requires
From us no other service than to keep   420
This one, this easy charge, of all the trees
In paradise that bear delicious fruit
So various, not to taste that only tree
Of knowledge, planted by the tree of life,
So near grows death to life, what e'er death is,   425
Some dreadful thing no doubt; for well thou know'st
God hath pronounced it death to taste that tree,
The only sign of our obedience left
Among so many signs of power and rule
Conferred upon us, and dominion given   430
Over all other creatures that possess
Earth, air, and sea. Then let us not think hard
One easy prohibition, who enjoy
Free leave so large to all things else, and choice
Unlimited of manifold delights: 435
But let us ever praise him, and extol
His bounty, following our delightful task
To prune these growing plants, and tend these flowers,
Which were it toilsome, yet with thee were sweet.'

        To whom thus Eve replied. 'O thou for whom   440
And from whom I was formed flesh of thy flesh,
And without whom am to no end, my guide
And head, what thou hast said is just and right.
For we to him indeed all praises owe,
And daily thanks, I chiefly who enjoy   445

419 Varied rhythms here; let them fluctuate.   **421** This *one*, this
easy…   **423 not to taste** at last we reach the prohibition, sinuously
emphasized.   **434 large** one of many 'big' words here; whole speech
contrasts with previous.   **440 for whom** cf 413. How do you respond
to the monosyllables, sounds etc of next few lines?

So far the happier lot, enjoying thee
Pre-eminent by so much odds, while thou
Like consort to thyself canst nowhere find.
    That day I oft remember, when from sleep
I first awaked, and found myself reposed   450
Under a shade on flowers, much wondering where
And what I was, whence thither brought, and how.
Not distant far from thence a murmuring sound
Of waters issued from a cave and spread
Into a liquid plain, then stood unmoved   455
Pure as the expanse of heaven; I thither went
With unexperienced thought, and laid me down
On the green bank, to look into the clear
Smooth lake, that to me seemed another sky.
As I bent down to look, just opposite,   460
A shape within the watery gleam appeared
Bending to look on me, I started back,
It started back, but pleased I soon returned,
Pleased it returned as soon with answering looks
Of sympathy and love; there I had fixed   465
Mine eyes till now, and pined with vain desire,
Had not a voice thus warned me, "What thou seest,
What there thou seest fair creature is thyself,
With thee it came and goes: but follow me,
And I will bring thee where no shadow stays   470
Thy coming, and thy soft embraces, he
Whose image thou art, him thou shall enjoy

447 odds extra, difference (17c usage). She has a superior husband; he can't find an equal wife.   **450 awaked** consider sensations of waking/sleeping used here for living/uncreated. At 458 sound and waters are confused; they come from a cave like a child from the womb; she goes to the pool to establish identity – give herself a mother? At any rate, a necessary rite of passage.   **462 started** jumped; rhetoric mimes mirroring. Based on myth of Narcissus: he did not return the love of Echo so she pined away into a disembodied voice; he then fell in love with his own reflection in a pool and he too pined to death and turned into a flower because he could not meet his image: Ovid *Metamorphoses* III. M is playing on Eve as self-image versus Adam's and God's image; and on Eve's self-concern in IX. But what's wrong with Narcissus?   **470 stays** waits for.

Inseparably thine, to him shalt bear
Multitudes like thyself, and thence be called
Mother of human race." What could I do,   475
But follow straight, invisibly thus led?
Till I espied thee, fair indeed and tall,
Under a platan, yet methought less fair,
Less winning soft, less amiably mild,
Than that smooth watery image; back I turned,   480
Thou following cried'st aloud, "Return fair Eve,
Whom fly'st thou? Whom thou fly'st, of him thou art,
His flesh, his bone; to give thee being I lent
Out of my side to thee, nearest my heart
Substantial life, to have thee by my side   485
Henceforth an individual solace dear;
Part of my soul I seek thee, and thee claim
My other half." With that thy gentle hand
Seized mine, I yielded, and from that time see
How beauty is excelled by manly grace   490
And wisdom, which alone is truly fair.'
    So spake our general mother, and with eyes
Of conjugal attraction unreproved,
And meek surrender, half embracing leaned
On our first father, half her swelling breast   495
Naked met his under the flowing gold
Of her loose tresses hid: he in delight
Both of her beauty and submissive charms
Smiled with superior love, as Jupiter
On Juno smiles, when he impregns the clouds   500
That shed May flowers; and pressed her matron lip
With kisses pure. Aside the devil turned

476 straight at once.   **478 platan** plane tree.   **486 individual** un-
dividable.   **492 general** mother of all people.   **493 unreproved**
unreprovable; innocent.   **499 Jupiter** king of gods, and sky; Juno
queen, and air; in mythology, the sky might impregnate the air so
that it brought forth creatures; and of course pregnant clouds bring rain
which brings fertility. The basic image is upper–lower; cf superior–
submissive, naked–hid and other pairs in this paragraph.   **501 matron**
married.

For envy, yet with jealous leer malign
Eyed them askance, and to himself thus plained.
  'Sight hateful, sight tormenting! Thus these two   505
Imparadised in one another's arms
The happier Eden, shall enjoy their fill
Of bliss on bliss, while I to hell am thrust,
Where neither joy nor love, but fierce desire,
Among our other torments not the least,   510
Still unfulfilled with pain of longing pines;
Yet let me not forget what I have gained
From their own mouths; all is not theirs it seems:
One fatal tree there stands of knowledge called,
Forbidden them to taste: knowledge forbidden?   515
Suspicious, reasonless. Why should their Lord
Envy them that? Can it be sin to know,
Can it be death? And do they only stand
By ignorance, is that their happy state,
The proof of their obedience and their faith?   520
O fair foundation laid whereon to build
Their ruin! Hence I will excite their minds
With more desire to know, and to reject
Envious commands, invented with design
To keep them low whom knowledge might exalt   525
Equal with gods; aspiring to be such,
They taste and die: what likelier can ensue?
  But first with narrow search I must walk round
This garden, and no corner leave unspied;
A chance but chance may lead where I may meet   530
Some wandering spirit of heaven, by fountain side,
Or in thick shade retired, from him to draw
What further would be learned. Live while ye may,
Yet happy pair; enjoy, till I return,
Short pleasures, for long woes are to succeed.'   535
  So saying, his proud step he scornful turned,
But with sly circumspection, and began
Through wood, through waste, o'er hill, o'er dale his roam.

517 Can it be sin to know? can it?   **519 that** sarcastic stress.

Mean while in utmost longitude, where heaven
With earth and ocean meets, the setting sun   540
Slowly descended, and with right aspéct
Against the eastern gate of paradise
Levelled his evening rays: it was a rock
Of alablaster, piled up to the clouds,
Conspicuous far, winding with one ascent   545
Accessible from earth, one entrance high;
The rest was craggy cliff, that overhung
Still as it rose, impossible to climb.
Betwixt these rocky pillars Gabriel sat
Chief of the angelic guards, awaiting night;   550
About him exercised heroic games
The unarmed youth of heaven, but nigh at hand
Celestial armoury, shields, helms, and spears,
Hung high with diamond flaming, and with gold.
Thither came Uriel, gliding through the even   555
On a sun beam, swift as a shooting star
In autumn thwart the night, when vapours fired
Impress the air, and shows the mariner
From what point of his compass to beware
Impertuous winds: he thus began in haste.   560
    'Gabriel, to thee thy course by lot hath given
Charge and strict watch that to this happy place
No evil thing approach or enter in;
This day at highth of noon came to my sphere
A spirit, zealous, as he seemed, to know   565
More of the almighty's works, and chiefly man
God's latest image: I described his way
Bent all on speed, and marked his airy gait;
But in the mount that lies from Eden north,

---

539 longitude west.   **541 with right aspéct** at right angles.   **544
alablaster** alabaster, a white marble.   **549 Gabriel** name means
might of God; one of the guardians of the 4 corners of the world. The
youth are his junior angel troops.   **555 Uriel** angel of the sun; he had
become suspicious of Satan after leaving him at III 735. His movement
'through' the evening seems to darken it.   **557 vapours fired** thought
that shooting stars were burning gases, that warned of bad weather. Cf
the expelling angels at XII 629.   **561 course** duty. Selected by casting lots.

Where he first lighted, soon discerned his looks   570
Alien from heaven, with passions foul obscured:
Mine eye pursued him still, but under shade
Lost sight of him; one of the banished crew
I fear, hath ventured from the deep, to raise
New troubles; him thy care must be to find.'   575
    To whom the wingèd warrior thus returned:
'Uriel, no wonder if thy perfect sight,
Amid the sun's bright circle where thou sit'st,
See far and wide: in at this gate none pass
The vigilance here placed, but such as come   580
Well known from heaven; and since meridian hour
No creature thence: if spirit of other sort,
So minded, have o'erleaped these earthy bounds
On purpose, hard thou know'st it to exclude
Spiritual substance with corporeal bar.   585
But if within the circuit of these walks,
In whatsoever shape he lurk, of whom
Thou tell'st, by morrow dawning I shall know.'

    So promised he, and Uriel to his charge
Returned on that bright beam, whose point now   590
    raised
Bore him slope downward to the sun now fallen
Beneath the Azores; whether the bright orb,
Incredible how swift, had thither rolled
Diurnal, or this less volúble earth
By shorter flight to the east, had left him there   595
Arraying with reflected purple and gold
The clouds that on his western throne attend:
Now came still evening on, and twilight grey

585 M has difficulties whenever the angels engage in epical activity such
as invasion or, as in v–vi, war. They are made of stuff (substance) but it
is so fluid and mobile that a physical obstacle (corporeal bar) can't stop it.
590 raised because sun now below horizon.   **594 Diurnal** in one day.
Cf the balanced argument about whether it is the sun or the earth that
moves at viii 122.   **volúble** rotating. The sun would have to go very
fast, the earth less.

Had in her sober livery all things clad;
Silence accompanied, for beast and bird, 600
They to their grassy couch, these to their nests
Were slunk, all but the wakeful nightingale;
She all night long her amorous descant sung;
Silence was pleased: now glowed the firmament
With living sapphires: Hesperus that led 605
The starry host, rode brightest, till the moon
Rising in clouded majesty, at length
Apparent queen unveiled her peerless light,
And o'er the dark her silver mantle threw.

When Adam thus to Eve: 'Fair consort, the hour 610
Of night, and all things now retired to rest
Mind us of like repose, since God hath set
Labour and rest, as day and night to men
Successive, and the timely dew of sleep
Now falling with soft slumbrous weight inclines 615
Our eyelids; other creatures all day long
Rove idle unemployed, and less need rest;
Man hath his daily work of body or mind
Appointed, which declares his dignity,
And the regard of heaven on all his ways; 620
While other animals unactive range,
And of their doings God takes no account.
To morrow ere fresh morning streak the east
With first approach of light, we must be risen,
And at our pleasant labour, to reform 625
Yon flowery arbours, yonder alleys green,
Our walk at noon, with branches overgrown,
That mock our scant manuring, and require
More hands than ours to lop their wanton growth:
These blossoms also, and those dropping gums, 630
That lie bestrown unsightly and unsmooth,

601 They...these former, latter. It is worth structuring this description
for such components as the bright, the silent, clothes... **605 Hesperus**
evening star, first to come out. **608 Apparent** clearly. **628 man-
uring** working with the hands, cultivation.

nature methodized ~ controlled

Ask riddance, if we mean to tread with ease;
Mean while, as nature wills, night bids us rest.'

   To whom thus Eve with perfect beauty adorned.
'My author and disposer, what thou bid'st   635
Unargued I obey; so God ordains,
God is thy law, thou mine: to know no more
Is woman's happiest knowledge and her praise.
   With thee conversing I forget all time,
All seasons and their change, all please alike.   640
Sweet is the breath of morn, her rising sweet,
With charm of earliest birds; pleasant the sun
When first on this delightful land he spreads
His orient beams, on herb, tree, fruit, and flower,
Glistering with dew; fragrant the fertile earth   645
After soft showers; and sweet the coming on
Of grateful evening mild, then silent night
With this her solemn bird and this fair moon,
And these the gems of heaven, her starry train:
   But neither breath of morn when she ascends   650
With charm of earliest birds, nor rising sun
On this delightful land, nor herb, fruit, flower,
Glistering with dew, nor fragrance after showers,
Nor grateful evening mild, nor silent night
With this her solemn bird, nor walk by moon,   655
Or glittering starlight without thee is sweet.
   But wherefore all night long shine these, for whom
This glorious sight, when sleep hath shut all eyes?'

   To whom our general ancestor replied.
'Daughter of God and man, accomplished Eve,   660
Those have their course to finish, round the earth,

635 author originator. **disposer** controller.   **639** The lyric is worth analysing; cf III 26, V 153. The line starting and ending with *sweet* is called the figure of epanalepsis; there are various other phrasal sortings. The return at 650 might be seen as the centre of the book, as parallel to Uriel's up-and-down sunbeam, and analogous to the sense of even(ing) balance generally.   **642 charm** birdsong.   **657** The first request for knowledge.   **660 accomplished** perfect.

By morrow evening, and from land to land
In order, though to nations yet unborn,
Ministering light prepared, they set and rise;
Lest total darkness should by night regain   665
Her old possession, and extinguish life
In nature and all things, which these soft fires
Not only enlighten, but with kindly heat
Of various influence foment and warm,
Temper or nourish, or in part shed down   670
Their stellar virtue on all kinds that grow
On earth, made hereby apter to receive
Perfection from the sun's more potent ray.
These then, though unbeheld in deep of night,
Shine not in vain, nor think, though men were none,   675
That heaven would want spectators, God want praise;
Millions of spiritual creatures walk the earth
Unseen, both when we wake, and when we sleep:
All these with ceaseless praise his works behold
Both day and night: how often from the steep   680
Of echoing hill or thicket have we heard
Celestial voices to the midnight air,
Sole, or responsive each to other's note
Singing their great creator: oft in bands
While they keep watch, or nightly rounding walk   685
With heavenly touch of instrumental sounds
In full harmonic number joined, their songs
Divide the night, and lift our thoughts to heaven.'

    Thus talking hand in hand alone they passed
On to their blissful bower; it was a place   690
Chosen by the sovereign planter, when he framed

665 darkness Chaos before creation II 962.   **671 kinds** species. Cosmic
generation is context for the first human nuptials.   **675 though men**
even if there weren't any men, that there would be nobody to look at
the sky.   **677 creatures** may suggest strange beings to us but in 17c
this phrase meant spiritual (as opposed to earthly) beings that God has
created. For Adam and Eve hearing angels singing cf Vaughan *Cor-
ruption*.   **689** Much information packed into line.

All things to man's delightful use; the roof
Of thickest covert was inwoven shade
Laurel and myrtle, and what higher grew
Of firm and fragrant leaf; on either side   695
Acanthus, and each odorous bushy shrub
Fenced up the verdant wall; each beauteous flower,
Iris all hues, roses, and jessamine
Reared high their flourished heads between, and wrought
Mosaic; underfoot the violet,   700
Crocus, and hyacinth with rich inlay
Broidered the ground, more coloured than with stone
Of costliest emblem: other creature here
Beast, bird, insect, or worm durst enter none;
Such was their awe of man. In shadier bower   705
More sacred and sequestered, though but feigned,
Pan or Silvanus never slept, nor nymph,
Nor Faunus haunted. Here in close recess
With flowers, garlands, and sweet-smelling herbs
Espousèd Eve decked first her nuptial bed,   710
And heavenly choirs the hymenéan sung,
What day the genial angel to our sire
Brought her in naked beauty more adorned,
More lovely than Pandora, whom the gods

696 **Acanthus** carvings of its leaves form capitals of Corinthian
columns. See other building words here. Note interwovenness of syntax.
699 **flourished** flowering.   700 **Mosaic** hard stress after 'wrought
[pause]'.   702 **Broidered** decorated, as a mosaic floor is with a pattern
or **emblem**, which might also be emblematic, symbolic (eg all three floor
flowers are blue, the colour of peace, prudence).   706 **feigned** fictional.
Consider effect here of all the negatives and er's.   707 **Pan** god of
nature; Silvanus of woods, gardens, boundaries; Faunus of forests. All
three depicted as hairy men with horns, goats' hindlegs and erect penises.
In myths they repeatedly pursue nymphs, the demi-goddesses of woods,
rivers etc. See Poussin.   708 **close recess** secret retreat.   711 **hy-
menéan** wedding hymn sung outside the door when bride and groom go
to bed. The herbs etc also normal for 17c weddings.   712 **genial** sug-
gests both a guardian angel, and an angel concerned with generation; odd
phrase, kind of palindrome. Actually it was God the Father who brought
them together according to Adam's story VIII 484; cf 476 here.   714
Pandora the first woman. Prometheus (forethought) had made a sort of
man and stole fire from heaven to give it life. Jove, angry at the theft, had
a woman made, and endowed with all gifts, by the gods. The gifts

Endowed with all their gifts, and O too like   715
In sad event, when to the unwiser son
Of Japhet brought by Hermes, she ensnared
Mankind with her fair looks, to be avenged
On him who had stole Jove's authentic fire.
   Thus at their shady lodge arrived, both stood,   720
Both turned, and under open sky adored
The God that made both sky, air, earth and heaven
Which they beheld, the moon's resplendent globe
And starry pole: 'Thou also mad'st the night,
Maker omnipotent, and thou the day,   725
Which we in our appointed work employed
Have finished happy in our mutual help
And mutual love, the crown of all our bliss
Ordained by thee, and this delicious place
For us too large, where thy abundance wants   730
Partakers, and uncropt falls to the ground.
But thou hast promised from us two a race
To fill the earth, who shall with us extol
Thy goodness infinite, both when we wake,
And when we seek, as now, thy gift of sleep.'   735
   This said unanimous, and other rites
Observing none, but adoration pure
Which God likes best, into their inmost bower
Handed they went; and eased the putting off
These troublesome disguises which we wear,   740
Straight side by side were laid, nor turned I ween

included beauty, and a box. The gods' messenger Hermes brought her to
Prometheus (who distrusted the gift and refused) and his brother Epi-
methus (after-thought) who, though warned, took her, and opened the
box: out flew all the evils the world has suffered ever since. The brothers
were the sons of Iapetus, who could be identified with Japhet, a son of
Noah. See D. and E. Panofksy *Pandora's box*.   **719 authentic** the fire
was sacred, and belonged essentially to Jove.   **721 open** puritans held
that you didn't have to be in church to worship the God who had *made* the
sky etc; cf 736.   **723 resplendent** literally.   **724 pole** vault of the
sky.   **732 race** normal for renaissance epithalamions to emphasize pro-
creation.   **735** I don't understand in what sense their children, yet un-
conceived, will go on praising God with them, in sleep as well as awake.
Spermatazoa and ova?   **741 ween** guess.

Adam from his fair spouse, nor Eve the rites
Mysterious of connubial love refused:
Whatever hypocrites austerely talk
Of purity and place and innocence,   745
Defaming as impure what God declares
Pure, and commands to some, leaves free to all.
Our maker bids increase, who bids abstain
But our destroyer, foe to God and man?

   Hail wedded love, mysterious law, true source   750
Of human offspring, sole propriety
In paradise of all things common else.
By thee adulterous lust was driven from men
Among the bestial herds to range, by thee
Founded in reason, loyal, just, and pure,   755
Relations dear, and all the charities
Of father, son, and brother first were known.
Far be it, that I should write thee sin or blame,
Or think thee unbefitting holiest place,
Perpetual fountain of domestic sweets,   760
Whose bed is undefiled and chaste pronounced,
Present, or past, as saints and patriarchs used.
Here Love his golden shafts employs, here lights
His constant lamp, and waves his purple wings,
Reigns here and revels; not in the bought smile   765

743 Mysterious as 312.   **745 place** fitting occasion. Marriage
had been regarded as impure by many authorities in the church,
so unlikely till after the fall; without the fall we would have gen-
erated by some touchless means. Still forbidden to Roman catholic
priests. Protestants defended it, even before the fall. Both sides
called on Bible texts for evidence.   **751 propriety** property. In
paradise there was no other kind of property. Interesting it now means
proper manners.   **754 bestial** M weak on animal behaviour.   **755
Founded** it is by marriage that loving relationships, and all the family
kinds of love, were first known; the reasonableness, loyalty etc may apply
either to marriage, or to the loves it introduced.   **760 domestic sweets**
home pleasures.   **762 used** some saints and all the grand old men of the
OT were married.   **763 Here** *here* – not in brothels or at court, with the
implication that whoring is the kind of love practised by the hypocrites
who object to it in Eden. The arrows, lamp etc belong to the conventional
figure of Eros presiding over fashionable poems and dances; M doesn't
however invent a new god of love here.

Of harlots, loveless, joyless, unendeared,
Casual fruition, nor in court amours
Mixed dance, or wanton mask, or midnight ball,
Or serenade, which the starved lover sings
To his proud fair, best quitted with disdain.   770
These lulled by nightingales embracing slept,
And on their naked limbs the flowery roof
Showered roses, which the morn repaired. Sleep on
Blest pair; and O yet happiest if ye seek
No happier state, and know to know no more.   775

    Now had night measured with her shadowy cone
Half way up hill this vast sublunar vault,
And from their ivory port the cherubim
Forth issuing at the accustomed hour stood armed
To their night watches in warlike parade,   780
When Gabriel to his next in power thus spake.
    'Uzziel, half these draw off, and coast the south
With strictest watch; these other wheel the north,
Our circuit meets full west.' As flame they part
Half wheeling to the shield, half to the spear.   785
From these, two strong and subtle spirits he called
That near him stood, and gave them thus in charge.
    'Ithuriel and Zephon, with winged speed

767 fruition copulation (a mildly obscene yet smart word at this
date; M plays on the degradation of its meaning). **768 Mixed**
men dancing with women. **769 starved** of love: attack on courtly
or romantic love. **775** No no no. **776 cone** the shadow of
night on the side of the earth opposite the sun, seen as a black
conical hat, its brim on the surface. Here the cone has moved 45°
up the night sky so it is 9 p.m. **778 port** gate. **780** Line drums:
night watch as in *war like*... **781 power** rank. The directions are
military, drawn from Roman (shield = left, spear = right) and 17c
militia drill. Also like stars: 'the vigilant patrol Of stars walks round about
the pole' in Marvell's *Appleton*. Note anti-rhyme 782–3. **782 Uzziel**
name of an angel in Hebrew tradition outside the Bible; means same as
Gabriel. Ithuriel = discovery of God, source uncertain; Zephon =
searcher of secrets *Numbers* xxvi. The point is that these characters are
closer to renaissance allegory than either biblical angels or Homeric
soldiers.

Search through this garden, leave unsearched no nook,
But chiefly where those two fair creatures lodge,   790
Now laid perhaps asleep secure of harm.
This evening from the sun's decline arrived
Who tells of some infernal spirit seen
Hitherward bent (who could have thought?) escaped
The bars of hell, on errand bad no doubt: 795
Such where ye find, seize fast, and hither bring.'
   So saying, on he led his radiant files,
Dazzling the moon; these to the bower direct
In search of whom they sought: him there they found
Squat like a toad, close at the ear of Eve;   800
Assaying by his devilish art to reach
The organs of her fancy, and with them forge
Illusions as he list, phantasms and dreams,
Or if, inspiring venom, he might taint
The animal spirits that from pure blood arise   805
Like gentle breaths from rivers pure, thence raise
At least distempered, discontented thoughts,
Vain hopes, vain aims, inordinate desires
Blown up with high conceits engendering pride.
Him thus intent Ithuriel with his spear   810
Touched lightly; for no falsehood can endure
Touch of celestial temper, but returns
Of force to its own likeness: up he starts

791 secure unanxious. Lullaby rhythm to line.   **793 Who** someone
arrived who.   **794 bent** directed.   **798 these** Ithuriel and Zephon,
while Gabriel leads his half on the northern patrol.   **800 toad**
many of the nightmare hybrids that represent devils, tempters and
especially lust are based on the toad in the painting of Bosch and in
various *Temptations of St Antony*. Thought poisonous. Posture coital; ear,
in dreams as analysed by Freud, often vaginal.   **801 Assaying** essaying,
trying, but also some sense of assay as in alchemy, black magic.   **802
fancy** imagination; Adam explains v 100. The waking fancy, working
properly, is controlled by reason. The organs don't seem to be anything
specific but the phrase intensifies the sexual ambiguity; cf notion of
breathing in venom.   **805 spirits** thin fluids supposed to derive from
blood and circulate through brain and nerves to make body move (animal
in this sense a creature with *anima*, soul, that moves). Straight physiology,
then suggesting temptation as a sort of flatulence of the nervous system.
812 temper manufacture.

Discovered and surprised. As when a spark
Lights on a heap of nitrous powder, laid   815
Fit for the tun some magazine to store
Against a rumoured war, the smutty grain
With sudden blaze diffused, inflames the air:
So started up in his own shape the fiend.
Back stept those two fair angels half amazed   820
So sudden to behold the grisly king;
Yet thus, unmoved with fear, accost him soon.
   'Which of those rebel spirits adjudged to hell
Com'st thou, escaped thy prison, and transformed,
Why sat'st thou like an enemy in wait   825
Here watching at the head of these that sleep?'
   'Know ye not then' said Satan, filled with scorn,
'Know ye not me? Ye knew me once no mate
For you, there sitting where ye durst not soar;
Not to know me argues your selves unknown,   830
The lowest of your throng; or if ye know,
Why ask ye, and superfluous begin
Your message, like to end as much in vain?'
   To whom thus Zephon, answering scorn with scorn.
'Think not, revolted spirit, thy shape the same,   835
Or undiminished brightness, to be known
As when thou stood'st in heaven upright and pure;
That glory then, when thou no more wast good,
Departed from thee, and thou resemblest now
Thy sin and place of doom obscure and foul.   840
But come, for thou, be sure, shalt give account
To him who sent us, whose charge is to keep
This place inviolable, and these from harm.'
   So spake the cherub, and his grave rebuke
Severe in youthful beauty, added grace   845

814 As when for epic similes see 159 and *PL : introduction* in
this series. The military technology runs through I–II, VI (469...),
X 272, 1073. **816 Fit** ready to be barrelled and stored in a maga-
zine. **818 diffused** when the gunpowder is expanded by the spark's
heat, it explodes. **819** Jerky stresses. Favourite moment for
illustrators, especially the romantic Burney, Fuseli, Runciman, Romney,
Barry.

Invincible: abashed the devil stood,
And felt how awful goodness is, and saw
Virtue in her shape how lovely, saw, and pined
His loss; but chiefly to find here observed
His lustre visibly impaired; yet seemed   850
Undaunted. 'If I must contend,' said he,
'Best with the best, the sender not the sent,
Or all at once; more glory will be won,
Or less be lost.' 'Thy fear,' said Zephon bold,
'Will save us trïal what the least can do   855
Single against thee wicked, and thence weak.'

  The fiend replied not, overcome with rage;
But like a proud steed reined, went haughty on,
Champing his iron curb: to strive or fly
He held it vain; awe from above had quelled   860
His heart, not else dismayed. Now drew they nigh
The western point, where those half-rounding guards
Just met, and closing stood in squadron joined
Awaiting next command. To whom their chief
Gabriel from the front thus called aloud.   865

  'O friends, I hear the tread of nimble feet
Hasting this way, and now by glimpse discern
Ithuriel and Zephon through the shade,
And with them comes a third of regal port,
But faded splendour wan; who by his gait   870
And fierce demeanour seems the prince of hell,
Not likely to part hence without contést;
Stand firm, for in his look defiance lours.'

  He scarce had ended, when those two approached
And brief related whom they brought, where found,   875
How busied, in what form and posture couched.

  To whom with stern regard thus Gabriel spake.
'Why hast thou, Satan, broke the bounds prescribed
To thy transgressions, and disturbed the charge
Of others, who approve not to transgress   880

869 **port** bearing.   876 **couched** as an animal lying in wait.

109

By thy example, but have power and right
To question thy bold entrance on this place;
Employed it seems to violate sleep, and those
Whose dwelling God hath planted here in bliss?'
    To whom thus Satan, with contemptuous brow.   885
'Gabriel, thou hadst in heaven the esteem of wise,
And such I held thee; but this question asked
Puts me in doubt. Lives there who loves his pain?
Who would not, finding way, break loose from hell,
Though thither doomed? Thou wouldst thy self, no doubt, 890
And boldly venture to whatever place
Farthest from pain, where thou might'st hope to change
Torment with ease, and soonest recompense
Dole with delight, which in this place I sought;
To thee no reason; who know'st only good,   895
But evil hast not tried: and wilt object
His will who bound us? Let him surer bar
His iron gates, if he intends our stay
In that dark durance: thus much what was asked.
The rest is true, they found me where they say;   900
But that implies not violence or harm.'
    Thus he in scorn. The warlike angel moved,
Disdainfully half smiling thus replied.
'O loss of one in heaven to judge of wise,
Since Satan fell, whom folly overthrew,   905
And now returns him from his prison 'scaped,
Gravely in doubt whether to hold them wise
Or not, who ask what boldness brought him hither
Unlicensed from his bounds in hell prescribed;
So wise he judges it to fly from pain   910
However, and to 'scape his punishment.
So judge thou still, presumptuous, till the wrath,
Which thou incurr'st by flying, meet thy flight
Sevenfold, and scourge that wisdom back to hell,

---

883 violate powerful language.   **886 esteem...** reputation of being
wise.   **888 who** anyone who.   **892 change...** exchange torture for
comfort.   **896 object** bring as an argument against me.   **902 moved**
angry.

Which taught thee yet no better, that no pain   915
Can equal anger infinite provoked.
But wherefore thou alone? Wherefore with thee
Came not all hell broke loose? Is pain to them
Less pain, less to be fled, or thou than they
Less hardy to endure? Courageous chief,   920
The first in flight from pain, hadst thou alleged
To thy deserted host this cause of flight,
Thou surely hadst not come sole fugitive.'
  To which the fiend thus answered frowning stern.
'Not that I less endure, or shrink from pain,   925
Insulting angel, well thou know'st I stood
Thy fiercest, when in battle to thy aid
The blasting vollied thunder made all speed
And seconded thy else not dreaded spear.
But still thy words at random, as before,   930
Argue thy inexperience what behoves
From hard assays and ill successes past
A faithful leader, not to hazard all
Through ways of danger by himself untried,
I therefore, I alone first undertook   935
To wing the desolate abyss, and spy
This new created world, whereof in hell
Fame is not silent, here in hope to find
Better abode, and my afflicted powers
To settle here on earth, or in mid air;   940
Though for possession put to try once more
What thou and thy gay legions dare against;
Whose easier business were to serve their Lord
High up in heaven, with songs to hymn his throne,
And practised distances to cringe, not fight.'   945

916 anger... the sense 'anger which becomes infinite when pro-
voked' is compressed into a syntactical mimesis. **928 thunder** the
rebel angels invent gunpowder and cannon in VI. **929 seconded** put
in second place; odd usage. **936** Satan quotes himself from II 404.
941 Though even if we have to fight you again, to gain earth. **942 gay**
echoes Mammon's criticisms of heaven (and Milton's of royal courts)
from II. 239. Gabriel returns criticism 958 and so perhaps confirms it.
945 distances courtly etiquette for when to bow etc – instead of the

To whom the warrior angel soon replied.
'To say and straight unsay, pretending first
Wise to fly pain, professing next the spy,
Argues no leader but a liar traced,
Satan, and couldst thou "faithful" add? O name,   950
O sacred name of faithfulness profaned!
Faithful to whom? To thy rebellious crew?
Army of fiends, fit body to fit head;
Was this your discipline and faith engaged,
Your military obedience, to dissolve   955
Allegiance to the acknowledged power supreme?
And thou sly hypocrite, who now wouldst seem
Patron of liberty, who more than thou
Once fawned, and cringed, and servilely adored
Heaven's awful monarch? Wherefore but in hope   960
To dispossess him, and thy self to reign?
But mark what I aread thee now, avaunt;
Fly thither whence thou fled'st: if from this hour
Within these hallowed limits thou appear,
Back to the infernal pit I drag thee chained,   965
And seal thee so, as henceforth not to scorn
The facile gates of hell too slightly barred.'
   So threatened he, but Satan to no threats
Gave heed, but waxing more in rage replied.
   'Then when I am thy captive talk of chains,   970
Proud limitary cherub, but ere then
Far heavier load thyself expect to feel
From my prevailing arm, though heaven's king
Ride on thy wings, and thou with thy compeers,
Used to the yoke, draw'st his triumphant wheels   975
In progress through the road of heaven star-paved.'
   While thus he spake, the angelic squadron bright
Turned fiery red, sharpening in moonèd horns

footwork of swordsmanship.   **949 traced** discovered.   **962 aread**
advise. Language here archaic.   **967 facile** he'll teach him not to scorn the
gates of hell for being too easy: they won't be.   **971 limitary** because
he guards the limits of paradise.   **976 progress** triumphal procession.
The lines echo Marlowe's *Tamburlaine*.

Their phalanx, and began to hem him round
With ported spears, as thick as when a field   980
Of Cerës ripe for harvest waving bends
Her bearded grove of ears, which way the wind
Sways them; the careful ploughman doubting stands
Lest on the threshing floor his hopeful sheaves
Prove chaff. On the other side Satan alarmed   985
Collecting all his might dilated stood,
Like Teneriff or Atlas unremoved:
His stature reached the sky, and on his crest
Sat horror plumed; nor wanted in his grasp
What seemed both spear and shield: now dreadful deeds 990
Might have ensued, nor only paradise
In this commotion, but the starry cope
Of heaven perhaps, or all the elements
At least had gone to wrack, disturbed and torn
With violence of this conflict, had not soon   995
The Eternal to prevent such horrid fray
Hung forth in heaven his golden scales, yet seen
Betwixt Astrea and the Scorpion sign,
Wherein all things created first he weighed,
The pendulous round earth with balanced air   1000
In counterpoise, now ponders all events,
Battles and realms: in these he put two weights
The sequel each of parting and of fight;
The latter quick up flew, and kicked the beam;

981 Cerës goddess of corn. The ploughman shifts the simile from
spears bristling like corn to daily life, and doubtful outcome; he recurs
at I 783 (another metamorphosis) and XII 631. But Satan blows himself up
like fabulous western mountains. **Teneriff** in the Canaries was thought
to be the highest in the world, perhaps 60 miles high; **Atlas** in
Morocco held up the sky and was named for a Titan who rebelled against
his god.   **987 unremoved** immovable. **989 horror** both something
that bristles, and that makes you shudder. Ancient helmets were crested
with feathers or animals. **990 seemed** because it's magical.   **992
cope** vault.   **997 scales** constellation Libra between Virgin and
Scorpion in zodiac; writing on the wall at Belshazzar's feast 'Mene
mene tekel upharsin' = thou art weighed in the balances and found
wanting *Daniel* v; and recurrence of IV's balancing imagery.   **1001
ponders** weighs, as well as considers.

Which Gabriel spying, thus bespake the fiend.　　　1005
　'Satan, I know thy strength, and thou know'st mine,
Neither our own but given; what folly then
To boast what arms can do, since thine no more
Than heaven permits, nor mine, though doubled now
To trample thee as mire: for proof look up,　　　1010
And read thy lot in yon celestial sign
Where thou art weighed, and shown how light, how weak,
If thou resist.' The fiend looked up and knew
His mounted scale aloft: nor more; but fled
Murmuring, and with him fled the shades of night.　　　1015

1005 bespake said to.　　**1012 weighed** most read it differently from
Gabriel, as meaning that to fight is worth less in God's will than to
separate.

Appendix to Book III

Invocation

Light

M offers three definitions of light; what would your own be?
Notice how many metaphors are based on it: 'to see the light',
'according to his lights', 'to stand in one's light', etc. Do our
criteria for defining a word differ from M's? The chief source for
the idea that God is light is the gospel of *John*, especially the first
chapter. It was most memorably rephrased by Dante in *Paradiso*
xxxiii:

> O abbondante grazia, ond' io presunsi
> ficcar lo viso per la luce eterna
> tanto che la veduta vi consunsi!
>
> Nel suo profondo vidi che s'interna,
> legato con amore in un volume,
> ciò che per l'universo si squaderna...
>
> A quella luce cotal si diventa,
> che volgersi da lei per altro aspetto
> è impossibil che mai si consenta.
>
> Però che il ben, ch' è del volero obbietto,
> tutto s'accoglie in lei, e fuor di quella
> è difettivo ciò che lì è perfetto...
>
> O luce eterna, che sola in te sidi,
> Sola t'intendi, e, da te intelletta
> ed intendente te, ami ed arridi!

O abounding grace, by which I dared to fix my look on the Eternal Light
so long that I spent all my sight upon it! In its depth I saw contained,
bound by love into a single book, that which is scattered in leaves through
the universe...At that light one is so transformed that he can never
consent to turn away to any other sight; for it completely sums up that
goodness which the will desires, and what is perfect there is defective
outside it...O Light Eternal, that alone abidest in thyself, alone knowest
thyself, and, known to thyself and knowing, lovest and smilest on thyself!

See also the final chorus of T. S. Eliot's *The rock*. The excitement
of the light–dark contrast is best brought out, musically, in the
opening of Haydn's *Creation*.

Light in paintings and architecture. 'The ascension of souls to paradise' from a diptych of *The last judgment* by Bosch (c. 1495) in Doge's palace, Venice. Cf treatments of light by Caravaggio (1573–1610), De la Tour (1593–1652), Rembrandt (1606–69), Vermeer (1632–75), Tiepolo (1696–1770) and the French impressionists. Kenneth Clark's *Civilization* 1969 has a chapter on 'The light of experience', dealing with the late 17c. Egyptian obelisks represented rays of the sun and were probably tipped with gold to catch the first morning light. Gold was a symbol of light in middle ages, both in mosaics and paintings. Why multicoloured stained glass in some churches, clear light in others? In the Ste Chapelle in Paris, one ascends from a dark lower chapel to an upper level which is almost all glass. Baroque churches often have a 'glory' behind the altar – a window designed to give effect of a sunburst. The most beautiful is Bernini's in St Peter's, Rome (1657–66). Ceilings of the same period (eg the church of the Gesù in Rome) are painted to give an illusion of opening into infinite space and radiant light. See also *Light from Aten to laser* (*Art news annual* xxxv) ed. T. B. Hess and John Ashbery 1969.

The underworld journey

See the references on Muses in the appendix to *PL* 1; also C. G. Jung on 'the Anima' in *Archetypes of the collective unconscious* 1959. The underworld journey is seen by Jungian psychologists as a symbol of our need to descend into the darker aspects of our nature before we can become fully human. These aspects include the trickster, the adventurer, the sacrificial victim and the 'shadow' – the dark side of the personality of which most people are unaware except when it appears in dreams. One patient undergoing analysis described a dream in which all four of these figures appeared, making him wonder which was to be 'the real hero'. Then he found himself at the beginning of a dangerous underworld journey:

We could get down by a small ladder, but I hesitate to do so because there are two young toughs standing by and I think that they will stop us. But when a woman in the group uses the ladder unmolested, I see that it is safe and all of us follow the woman down.

The analyst's comment was:

For most people the dark or negative side of the personality remains unconscious. The hero, on the contrary, must realize that the shadow exists and that he can draw strength from it... The saving elements in the dream are the man-made ladder, which here is probably a symbol of the rational mind, and the presence of the woman who encourages the dreamer to use it. Her appearance in the final sequence of the dream points to a psychic need to include a feminine principle as a complement to all this excessively masculine activity.

J. L. HENDERSON Ancient myths and modern man in
Man and his symbols ed. C. G. Jung, Dell; Aldus Books 1964

At various times in *PL* Satan seems to play the roles of trickster, adventurer, and even self-sacrificing idealist. Is he also Milton's shadow? Do these versions of the 'true hero' throw any light on the question 'Who is the hero of *PL*?'

Blindness

Other passages where M speaks personally of his blindness are *Sonnets* XVI, XIX, 'To Mr. Cyriack Skinner upon his blindness', and *Defensio secunda* 1654:

Why should I not bear what every man ought to be ready to bear calmly if it happens – what I know may happen to any human being and has indeed happened to some of the best and most famous men in history? Or shall I recall those old poets and sages of the distant past whose misfortunes the gods are said to have recompensed with far more powerful gifts and whom men so respected that they preferred to blame the gods themselves rather than associate their blindness with crime?...For my part, God (who knows my heart and all my thoughts) is my witness that, though I have questioned myself over and over and searched all the corners of my life, I am conscious of no action either recent or remote whose wickedness might justify such a great misfortune...We blind men are surely not the least of God's concerns, for he looks the more mercifully and graciously upon us, the less able we are to see anything but himself. Woe to the man who mocks or harms us! He deserves a public curse. Divine law and favour have made us not only safe from men's injuries, but almost sacred, and the shades around us seem created not by the weakness of our eyes but by the shadow of angel wings. Divine favour, moreover, often lights up these shadows – with an inner light, far more lasting.

But cf *Samson agonistes* 80. See also *The story of my life* by Helen Keller 1903 and her prose poem *A hymn to darkness* in *The world I live in* 1933; *The gifts* by Jorge Luis Borges (b. 1899, trans. Irving Feldman 1968); and *Prayer to St Lucy* by John Heath-Stubbs (b. 1918); Poussin's *Blind Orion in search of the rising sun* 1658, in the Louvre; Michelangelo's *Conversion of St Paul* Vatican 1542–5.

God

The most interesting religious poets to compare with Milton are
Donne, Herbert, and Hopkins. See also Browning's *Caliban upon
Setebos; or natural theology in the island* 1864 and Louis Mac-
Neice's *London rain* 1939. God's ways to men are most searchingly
discussed in *Job*. See Blake's illustrations to it, and two modern
reinterpretations, *The masque of reason* 1945 by Robert Frost and
J.B. by Archibald MacLeish (b. 1892). C. G. Jung wrote *An
answer to Job* 1952, trans. in *Psychology and religion* 1958.

But what do I love when I love my God? Not material beauty or beauty of
a temporal order; not the brilliance of earthly light, so welcome to our eyes;
not the sweet melody of harmony and song; not the fragrance of flowers,
perfumes and spices; not manna or honey; not limbs such as the body
delights to embrace. It is not these that I love when I love my God. And
yet, when I love him, it is true that I love a light of a certain kind, a voice,
a perfume, a food, an embrace; but they are of the kind that I love in my
inner self, when my soul is bathed in light that is not bound by space;
when it listens to sound that never dies away; when it breathes fragrance
that is not borne away on the wind; when it tastes food that is never con-
sumed by the eating; when it clings to an embrace from which it is not
severed by fulfilment of desire. This is what I love when I love my God.
ST AUGUSTINE from *Confessions* AD 397–8 trans.
R. S. Pine-Coffin, Faber 1961

[George is dictating a lecture.]
George. To ask, 'Is God?' appears to presuppose a Being who perhaps
isn't. . .and thus is open to the same objection as the question, 'Does God
exist?'. . .but until the difficulty is pointed out it does not have the same
propensity to confuse language with meaning and to conjure up a God
who may have any number of predicates including omniscience, perfec-
tion and four-wheel-drive but not, as it happens, existence. . .And then
again, I sometimes wonder whether the question ought not to be, 'Are
God?' Because it is to account for two quite unconnected mysteries that
the human mind looks beyond humanity and it is two of him that philo-
sophy obligingly provides. There is, first, the God of Creation to account
for existence, and, second, the God of Goodness to account for moral
values. I say they are unconnected because there is no logical reason why
the fountain-head of goodness in the universe should have necessarily
created the universe in the first place; nor is it necessary, on the other
hand, that a Creator should care tuppence about the behaviour of his
creations. . .we find these two independent mysteries: the how and the
why of the overwhelming question:
Dotty. (off): Is anybody there?
George. (pause): Perhaps all mystical experience is a form of coincidence.
Or vice versa, of course.   TOM STOPPARD from *Jumpers* Faber 1972

The idea of God is an absolutely necessary psychological function of an
irrational nature, which has nothing whatever to do with the question of

God's existence. The human intellect can never answer this question, still less give any proof of God. Moreover such proof is superfluous, for the idea of an all-powerful divine Being is present everywhere, unconsciously if not consciously, because it is an archetype...I therefore consider it wiser to acknowledge the idea of God consciously; for, if we do not, something else is made God, usually something quite inappropriate and stupid such as only an 'enlightened' intellect could hatch forth.

C. G. JUNG from *The personal and the collective unconscious* in *The psychology of the unconscious* trans. B. M. Hinkle, Routledge and Kegan Paul 1919

> O more exceeding love or law more just?
> Just law indeed, but more exceeding love!

Here in the *Circumcision ode* Milton, like the angels in *Paradise Lost*, acclaims the victory of ἀγάπη over law; but the carefully balanced rhetoric puts them back into an equation. Behind this and our objection lie two historical ideals of fatherhood: one in which the father is utterly reliable in his justice, but calculating even in his love; the other in which he is less predictable, but warm. The perfect father would be spontaneous and reliable; Milton's lacks a spontaneity equal to his reliability and it is because we are bound to see him – poetically and theologically – as an ideal parent that we object and cannot be soothed by theory.

J. B. BROADBENT from *Some graver subject* Chatto and Windus 1960

Those who insist upon a liberal democratic reading of the poem are outraged by God the Father, his cruelty, his pedantic notions of freedom and justice. But...without the arbitrary there cannot be religion; or at least there cannot be religion as distinct from the prompting of our sensibility. There can only be religion which accommodates itself to our desires. There is merit in obeying a just command, but it is not the same merit as that of obeying an unjust command: the one is a matter of genial relationships, the other is the last sacrifice. I believe because it is impossible, I obey without question. Those who go out of their way to make a case for God in *Paradise Lost* by somehow squaring his acts with the human idea of fair play are misguided, because the laws of fair dealing do not apply.

DENIS DONOGHUE from *God with thunder* in his *Thieves of fire* Faber 1973

See *Exodus* xx 1–6, the York Last Judgment play, Thomas Hardy *A plaint to man* 1909–10, and Stevie Smith (d. 1972) *God speaks*.

Free will and predestination

This issue is still very much alive, in such phrases as 'I couldn't help it', 'You'll always be a bourgeois', 'I'll never be able to love anyone because I had an unhappy childhood.' Try to trace the causes of *one* act of yours as far back as you can go. Which is freer, an act whose cause you don't understand, or one which you can explain completely? For the effects of the presbyterian belief in predestination at its most chilling see Burns (1759–96) *Holy Willie's prayer* and James Hogg's *Confessions of a justified sinner* 1824, and compare Tennyson *St Simeon Stylites* 1842 and Browning *Johannes Agricola in meditation* 1855. Modern novels exploring the theme of freedom include Jean-Paul Sartre *The roads to freedom* 1945 (only three of four projected volumes published yet), William Golding *Free fall* 1959, and almost any Iris Murdoch novel.

Thus he not only shows mercy as he chooses, but also makes men stubborn as he chooses. You will say, 'Then why does God blame a man? For who can resist his will?' Who are you, sir, to answer God back? Can the pot speak to the potter and say, 'Why did you make me like this?' Surely the potter can do what he likes with the clay. Is he not free to make out of the same lump two vessels, one to be treasured, the other for common use?

Romans ix

'Why, then, do you insist that all that is scanned by the sight of God becomes necessary? Men see things but this certainly doesn't make them necessary. And your seeing them doesn't impose any necessity on the things you see present, does it?'
'No.'
'And if human and divine present may be compared, just as you see certain things in this your present time, so God sees all things in His eternal present. So that this divine foreknowledge does not change the nature and property of things; it simply sees things present to it exactly as they will happen at some time as future events.'

BOETHIUS from *The consolation of philosophy* c. AD 524
trans. Watts, Penguin 1959

Before the first man was created, God in his eternal counsel had determined what he willed to be done with the whole human race.

In the hidden counsel of God it was determined that Adam should fall from the unimpaired condition of his nature, and by his defection should involve all his posterity in sentence of eternal death.

Upon the same decree depends the distinction between elect and reprobate: as he adopted some for himself for salvation, he destined others for eternal ruin...

While the will of God is the supreme and primary cause of all things and God holds the devil and the godless subject to his will, nevertheless God cannot be called the cause of sin, nor the author of evil, nor subject of any guilt.

CALVIN from *Articles concerning predestination* c. 1550

Tuesday 10 October 1769: Dr. Johnson shunned tonight any discussion of the perplexed question of fate and free will, which I attempted to agitate. 'Sir, (said he) we *know* our will is free, and *there's* an end on't.'

BOSWELL from *Life of Johnson* 1791

[The Grand Inquisitor accuses Christ:]
Didst thou forget that man prefers peace, and even death, to freedom of choice in the knowledge of good and evil?... Thou didst desire man's free

love, that he should follow Thee freely, enticed and taken captive by Thee. In place of the rigid, ancient law, man must hereafter with free heart decide for himself what is good and what is evil, having only Thy image before him as his guide. But didst Thou not know he would at last reject even Thy image and Thy truth, if he is weighed down with the fearful burden of free choice?

DOSTOYEVSKY from *The brothers Karamazov* 1880
trans. Constance Garnett 1912

Freedom is not a reward or a decoration that is celebrated with champagne...Oh, no! It's a chore, on the contrary, and a long-distance race, quite solitary and very exhausting. No champagne, no friends raising their glasses as they look at you affectionately. Alone in a forbidding room, alone in the prisoner's box before the judges, and alone to decide in face of oneself or in the face of others' judgement. At the end of all freedom is a court sentence; that's why freedom is too heavy to bear.

ALBERT CAMUS from *The fall* 1956
trans. J. O'Brien, Hamish Hamilton 1957

The Son and redemption

Art. See two illustrations to *PL* – Hogarth's *The council in heaven* c. 1724 and Blake's *Christ offering to redeem man* 1807 – reproduced in Pointon *M and English art* 1970. There are innumerable depictions of crucifixions and martyrdoms; at opposite extremes, see *The last communion and martyrdom of St Denis* by Bellechose (d. 1444) in the Louvre (the saint's sufferings and Christ's shown concurrently, in gory detail) and Bernini's statue of St Teresa being pierced by an angel with a flaming dart (Santa Maria della Vittoria, Rome), and compare, for a similar blend of religious and sexual feeling, Crashaw's *Hymn to St Teresa* and Albee's *Tiny Alice*. Perhaps it was his distaste for this sort of almost sadistic dwelling on suffering that made Milton avoid dealing directly with the crucifixion theme.

Music. Handel's *Messiah* (contains most biblical prophecies of Christ); Bach's *St Matthew* and *St John passions*.

Some views on redemption and grace

The Adam–Christ parallel is memorably put in Donne's *Hymn to God, my God, in my sickness*. Pre-Christian prophetic works mention a healing tree, apparently a counterpart to the fatal one in Eden, and it is mentioned again in the apocryphal *Gospel of Nicodemus* as Adam and the rest of mankind are waiting in hell for Christ to come down and redeem them:

Then Seth drew near unto the holy patriarchs and prophets, and said, 'When I, Seth, was praying at the gates of paradise, behold Michael the angel of the Lord appeared unto me, saying: I am sent unto thee from the Lord: it is I that am set over the body of man. And I say unto thee, Seth, vex not thyself with tears, praying and entreating for the oil of the tree of mercy, that thou mayest anoint thy father Adam for the pain of his body: for thou wilt not be able to receive it save in the last days and times... Then shall the most beloved Son of God, even Christ Jesus, come down upon the earth and shall bring in our father Adam into paradise unto the tree of mercy.'   *The Gospel of Nicodemus* part II, iii

Edward. Do you mean that having chosen this form of death
          She did not suffer as ordinary people suffer?
Reilly.   Not at all what I meant. Rather the contrary.
          I'd say that she suffered all that we should suffer
          In fear and pain and loathing – all these together –
          And reluctance of the body to become a *thing*.
          I'd say she suffered more, because more conscious
          Than the rest of us. She paid the highest price
          In suffering. That is part of the design.
                    T. S. ELIOT from *The cocktail party* Faber 1950

For Milton's own concept of Christ, see the *Nativity ode*, the unfinished *Passion* and above all *Paradise regained*.

Heaven

Englishmen of Milton's time liked to derive this word either from 'heaving' (the rolling of the spheres) or from 'haven' (cf Hopkins' poem *Heaven-haven*). Outside the Christian tradition, there are three kinds of heaven. (1) The home of the gods, above the earth and usually out of bounds to mortals. The Greek and Roman gods were thought of as happy and therefore, it was argued, they couldn't take an interest in affairs below (cf the end of Tennyson's *Lotus-eaters*). (2) The home of dead mortals, in which they retain their individuality. Sometimes a sort of fairyland. On or under the earth, but often in a different dimension of time. Can be associated with rewards and punishments. (3) A state in which the individual personality is annihilated in mystic union with the infinite (eg the Hindu Nirvana).

The Christian heaven combines (1) and (2) ((3) has never been popular in the West): angels can take on human form and human beings can become divine. Milton seems sometimes to have had difficulty reconciling the happiness of the angels with their interest in potentially depressing human events – eg, when news of man's fall reaches heaven displeased

> All were who heard, dim sadness did not spare
> That time celestial visages, yet mixed
> With pity, violated not their bliss.   X 22–5

[the Elysian fields]

> the Happy Place, the green and genial
> Glades where the fortunate live, the home of the blessed spirits.
> What largesse of bright air, clothing the vales in dazzling
> Light, is here! This land has a sun and stars of its own.
> Some exercise upon the grassy playing-fields
> Or wrestle on the yellow sands in rivalry of sport;
> Some foot the rhythmic dances and chant poems aloud.
> VIRGIL from *The Aeneid* VI trans C. Day Lewis, Oxford U.P. 1952
> Cf *PL* II 521 ff

[the earthly paradise]

> The soil thereof most fragrant flowers did yield,
> Like rubies, gold, pearls, sapphires, topaz stones,
> Chrysolites, diamonds, jacints for the nones.
>
> The trees that there did grow were ever green,
> The fruits that thereon grew were never fading,
> The sundry colour'd birds did sit between,
> And sung most sweet, the fruitful boughs them shading:
> The rivers clear as crystal to be seen,
> The fragrant smell the sense and soul invading,
> With air so temperate and so delightsome,
> As all the place beside was clear and lightsome.
> ARIOSTO from *Orlando furioso* XXXIV trans. Harington 1591

See also Southwell (d. 1595) *Flowers of heaven*, the end of Crashaw's *Hymn to St Teresa* 1646, and *Peace* by Vaughan (d. 1695). Other literary treatments are described in H. R. Patch *The other world* 1950, visual interpretations in R. Hughes *Heaven and hell in western art* 1968. Much romantic music aims for a 'heavenly' effect: eg Wagner's Valhalla music in *Rheingold* and the end of Mahler's *Eighth symphony*, a setting of the last scene of Goethe's *Faust*.

The paradise of fools

For the long tradition of vulgar anti-clerical satire see eg Boccaccio's *Decameron* and the Friar's and Summoner's tales from *The Canterbury tales* of Chaucer (d. 1400). The grotesqueness and monstrosity of the inhabitants of Milton's false paradise are reminiscent of medieval depictions of hell and devils all falling over each other in a heap. See Hughes *Heaven and hell in western art*; bellows and bagpipe frequently appear as symbols of folly. Compare Bosch's *Cart of hay* and *Ship of fools*, Breughel's *Tower of Babel* and *Parable of the blind*, also Hogarth's engravings: *Some of the principal inhabitants of the moon* 1725 and *Credulity, superstition and fanaticism* 1762.

Satan enters the universe

On ragged black sails
he soars hovering over
everything and death;
a blight in the eye
of the stunning sun.

DOUGLAS LIVINGSTONE (b. 1932) from *Vulture* Oxford U.P.

On a starred night Prince Lucifer uprose.
Tired of his dark dominion swung the fiend
Above the rolling ball in cloud part screened,
Where sinners hugged their spectre of repose.
Poor prey to his hot fit of pride were those.
And now upon his western wing he leaned,
Now his huge bulk o'er Afric's sands careened,
Now the black planet shadowed Arctic snows.
Soaring through wider zones that pricked his scars
With memory of the old revolt from Awe,
He reached a middle height, and at the stars,
Which are the brain of heaven, he looked, and sank.
Around the ancient track marched, rank on rank,
The army of unalterable law.

GEORGE MEREDITH (d. 1909) *Lucifer in starlight*

Jacob's ladder. There are many illustrations of this subject (the earliest – showing a plain wooden ladder – was traced on a wall in the Catacombs). See eg paintings by Ribera and Murillo and Blake's watercolour of *Jacob's dream*. Schoenberg wrote an unfinished oratorio about it. Ladders were thought to link earth with heaven, death with life: miniature ones were buried with Egyptian pharaohs. They are difficult to climb, so they can symbolize the difficult route to heaven.

The third-century *Vision of Perpetua* speaks of a golden ladder stretching to Heaven from earth, each of whose thousand steps is guarded with hooks and sharp knives. If a wicked man treads on one, the cutters go to work on him and he falls into the clutches of an enormous dragon which lies coiled round the ladder's base...Ladders were normally used in art as symbols of moral improvement. The soul's ascent, rung by rung, away from the earth, fitted neatly into the Platonic cosmos with its concentric spheres of perfection, rising from earth to *Primum Mobile*. But quite often the ladder is depicted simply as a trial, with demons and angels flitting about it, the former dragging sinners down into the pit of Hell, the latter keeping the feet of the virtuous on the rungs and directing their eyes to Heaven.

ROBERT HUGHES from *Heaven and hell in western art*
Weidenfeld & Nicolson 1968

The book reproduces a 7c *Ladder of judgment* of this type. In the *Paradiso*, Dante climbs a ladder which extends from the starry sphere up to heaven and which symbolizes contemplation. Theologically, Christ was identified with the ladder, since his incarnation linked heaven and earth. Alchemically, it represented the scale from matter to spirit and the possibility of transformation, which Jung also finds implied by the ladder images in the dreams of his patients (see *Psychology and alchemy* 1944 trans. 1953). For other interpretations, see Wordsworth *Composed upon an evening of extraordinary splendour and beauty* 1818 and Denise Levertov *The Jacob's ladder* 1962.

Astronomy. Besides the works quoted, see A. J. Meadows *The high firmament, a survey of astronomy in English literature* 1969, Marjorie Nicolson *Voyages to the moon* 1948 and *The breaking of the circle* 1960 and Hugh Kearney *Science and change 1500–1700* 1971. For the change v. permanence paradox, Spenser's *Mutability cantos* (c. 1596). Readers of science fiction will have less trouble than most in imagining the strange perspectives and angles of vision in this part of the poem; there are also some interesting variations on them in John Collier *PL: a screenplay for the cinema of the mind* 1973. The theme of discovering an unfallen planet has intrigued a number of writers since the seventeenth century: eg James Blish *A case of conscience* 1959 and C. S. Lewis *Perelandra* 1943 (the second part of a trilogy, also published as *Voyage to Venus*).

The sun

For sun-worship in its modern form see the D. H. Lawrence short stories *The woman who rode away* and *Sun*, also:

All existence is dual, and surging towards a consummation into being. In the seed of the dandelion, as it floats with its little umbrella of hairs, sits the Holy Ghost in tiny compass. The Holy Ghost is that which holds the light and the dark, the day and the night, the wet and the sunny, united in one little clue. There it sits, in the seed of the dandelion.

The seed falls to earth. The Holy Ghost rouses, saying '*Come!*' And out of the sky come the rays of the sun, and out of the earth comes damp-ness and dark and the death-stuff. They are called in, like those bidden to a feast. The sun sits down at the hearth, inside the seed; and the dark, damp death-returner sits on the opposite side, with the host between. And the host says to them: '*Come! Be merry together!*' So the sun looks with desirous curiosity on the dark face of the earth, and the dark damp one looks with wonder on the bright face of the other, who comes from the sun. And the host says: '*Here you are at home. Lift me up, between you, that I may cease to be a Ghost. For it longs me to look out, it longs me to dance with the dancers.*'

So the sun in the seed, and the earthly one in the seed take hands, and laugh, and begin to dance.

Reflections on the death of a porcupine 1925

Heat and pressure maintain the constant sun on which our lives depend. But this fiery furnace at the core of the sun, so much fiercer and more awe-inspiring than any imagined Hell, also holds the secret of the solar energy which men for so long worshipped with an intuitive awareness of their utter dependence upon it. In the heat and pressure of the sun's heart almost all the atoms are shattered, the electrons torn from their nuclei and all alike freed to roam and so to keep this core gaseous in spite of the colossal pressure. In these conditions one process continues steadily. It is the transformation of the elements sought by the alchemists with their pathetic little flames and retorts. A tiny fraction of the star's vast stock of hydrogen is everlastingly being turned into helium.

JACQUETTA HAWKES from *Man and the sun* Random House 1962

Tampering with nature, especially by means of fire, has always been regarded as suspect. Hence smiths, like alchemists, are sinister figures of folklore. See Mircea Eliade *The forge and the crucible* 1962. Mammon in *The fairy queen* II vii is both a smith and a symbol of Satan tempting Christ with the offer of power and wealth. And see Ezra Pound's *The alchemist* 1912, 'a chant for the transmutation of metals'. There are many paintings of alchemists by David Teniers the younger (1610–94). See also the illustrations to Jung's *Psychology and alchemy* 1944 trans. 1953, a fascinating interpretation of alchemical symbolism as an unconscious expres-sion of man's search for wholeness and self-realization.

Uriel. For the sort of angel Milton may have been imagining in his descriptions of Uriel and the disguised Satan, see Botticini *Tobias and the three angels* c. 1467 (the Uffizi, Florence) – based on the Apocryphal *Book of Tobit* – which shows curly-haired angels in both military and civilian dress. Literature of angels: R. H. West *Milton and the angels* 1955; Spenser *Fairy queen* II viii; Tasso's description of Gabriel in *Jerusalem delivered* I; Prologue in heaven from Goethe's *Faust* part I; Emerson's satiric poem *Uriel*.

Appendix to Book IV

Milton's 'argument'

Satan now in prospect of Eden, and nigh the place where he must now attempt the bold enterprise which he undertook alone against God and man, falls into many doubts with himself, and many passions, fear, envy, and despair; but at length confirms himself in evil, journeys on to paradise, whose outward prospect and situation is described, overleaps the bounds, sits in the shape of a cormorant on the tree of life, as the highest in the garden to look about him. The garden described; Satan's first sight of Adam and Eve; his wonder at their excellent form and happy state, but with resolution to work their fall; overhears their discourse, thence gathers that the tree of knowledge was forbidden them to eat of, under penalty of death; and thereon intends to found his temptation, by seducing them to transgress: then leaves them a while to know farther of their state by some other means. Mean while, Uriel descending on a sunbeam warns Gabriel, who had in charge the gate of paradise, that some evil spirit had escaped the deep, and passed at noon by his sphere in the shape of a good angel down to paradise, discovered after by his furious gestures in the mount. Gabriel promises to find him ere morning. Night coming on, Adam and Eve discourse of going to their rest: their bower described; their evening worship. Gabriel drawing forth his bands of night-watch to walk the round of paradise, appoints two strong angels to Adam's bower, lest the evil spirit should be there doing some harm to Adam or Eve sleeping; there they find him at the ear of Eve, tempting her in a dream, and bring him, though unwilling, to Gabriel; by whom questioned, he scornfully answers, prepares resistance, but hindered by a sign from heaven, flies out of paradise.

What primeval man portrayed as his own image upon the walls of the caverns or upon carved bones appears barely human to our eyes. He is very far removed from the narcissism of a creature enamoured of his own beauty, as the Greeks taught us to see ourselves. Primeval man depicts himself in no way as self-assured, self-reliant, and superior...The human figure appeared but sporadically: usually naked; the face veiled; the head sometimes lacking altogether, sometimes bent forward like an animal's, or, most usually, depicted as the head of an animal...the figure of the human being appeared negligible in comparison with the beauty and strength of animal figures.

S. GIEDION *The eternal present: the beginnings of art. A contribution on constancy and change* Oxford U.P. 1962

The key to man's nature lies in his evolution of social hunting; like the dog, man was a social carnivore...the actions of every individual affected others in the social group...It is the conflict between the two needs, those of the individual and those of the society, that makes necessary some device for directing a choice between possible actions...That is why the story of Adam and Eve has been described by religious teachers as the 'fall of man' and by psychologists as the coming of self-consciousness and self-awareness...Clearly, the evolution of self-awareness brought with it a totally new and terrible situation: that human activity was to be directed, not by the straightforward operations of an unthinking brain...but by the conscious functioning of the human mind...Self-consciousness and foresight therefore brought discord to the mind of man...The theory of evolution makes it clear that the functional unit in this dynamic process is not the individual but the population...The division of labor between the sexes...is the beginning of the process of individualization...The wife and husband recognized each other as economic and sexual partners. The frontal position in coitus enhanced this recognition; role names, such as 'wife', 'husband', 'father', 'mother', appeared and reflected the division of labor within the family...Individualization appears to have grown through the recognition of an individual's dependence on other particular individuals...But besides the division of labor there was possibly a more fundamental reason for the individualization of *Homo sapiens*. The more behavior depends on learning and the more complex it becomes, the more behavior will vary among individuals...The individual, as the source of invention, is the source of culture.

> BERNARD G. CAMPBELL *Human evolution: an introduction to man's adaptations* Heinemann Educational 1967

For a fiction on early man, and an allegory of original sin in terms of interbreeding with Neanderthal man, see William Golding *The inheritors* 1955.

The best introduction to the theological themes of *PL* IV, such as innocence and guilt, is Wallace Stevens' meditation on it, *Sunday morning* (1928).

A fall of some sort or other – the creation, as it were, of the non-absolute – is the fundamental postulate of the moral history of man. Without this hypothesis, man is unintelligible; with it, every phenomenon is explicable. The mystery itself is too profound for human insight.

> COLERIDGE *Table talk* 1 May 1830

Though Christian theology has frequently expressed the idea of the total depravity of man in extravagant terms, it has never been without witness to the fact that human sin cannot destroy the essential character of man...Christian theology has found it difficult to reconcile the rationalistic rejection of the myth of the Fall without falling into the literalistic error of insisting upon the Fall as an historical event. One of the consequences of this literalism...is the assumption that the perfection from which man fell is to be assigned to a particular historical period, *i.e.* the paradisaical period before the Fall. This chronological interpretation of a relation which cannot be expressed in terms of time without being falsified must not be attributed to the authority of the Biblical myth alone.

The Stoics, after all, also believed in a golden age of innocency at the beginning of the world and thought that the equality and liberty which their natural law enjoined, but which were beyond the possibilities of actual history, were realities of that blessed period. Furthermore every individual is inclined to give a chronological and historical version of the contrast between what he is and what he ought to be; for he regards the innocency of his childhood as a symbol and a reminder of his true nature.

REINHOLD NIEBUHR *The nature and destiny of man: a Christian interpretation* 2 vols Nisbet 1941 vol. I, chap 10

The fallen nature of modern man cannot be separated from social progress. On the one hand the growth of economic productivity furnishes the conditions for a world of greater justice; on the other hand it allows the technical apparatus and the social groups which administer it a disproportionate superiority to the rest of the population...Even though the individual disappears before the apparatus which he serves, that apparatus provides for him as never before. In an unjust state of life, the impotence and pliability of the masses grow with the quantitative increase in commodities allowed them...The flood of detailed information and candyfloss entertainment simultaneously instructs and stultifies mankind.

MAX HORKHEIMER and THEODOR W. ADORNO *Dialectic of enlightenment* 1944 rev. 1947. trans. John Cumming, Herder & Herder, New York 1972

As in the earliest days of the movement [the heretical Brethren of the Free Spirit who ranged across Europe in the 14c], one expression of this attitude was still [in later developments] a promiscuous and mystically coloured eroticism...From the Swabian heretics in the thirteenth century down to the Ranters in the seventeenth the same view is expressed again and again: for the 'subtle in spirit' sexual intercourse cannot under any circumstances be sinful...The *Homines intelligentiae* called the act 'the delight of Paradise'...In this context the Adam-cult which is frequently found amongst the adepts of the Free Spirit becomes perfectly comprehensible...the adepts did at times practise ritual nakedness...asserting – as one inquisitor put it – that they were restored to the state of innocence which had existed before the Fall...one can already recognize in this medieval heresy that blend of millenarianism and primitivism which has become one of the commoner forms of modern romanticism. In the Adam-cult the lost Paradise was recreated and at the same time the advent of the Millennium was affirmed.

NORMAN COHN *The pursuit of the millennium: revolutionary millenarians and mystical anarchists of the Middle Ages* Granada 1957

Cf Broadbent 'The image of God or two yards of skin' in *The body as a medium of expression*: ed. Jonathan Benthall and Ted Polhemus 1975.

In Hesiod['s version of the Pandora myth: *Theogony* trans. N. O. Brown Indianapolis 1953] Zeus, a rancorous and arbitrary father figure, is sending Epimetheus evil in the form of female genitalia, is actually chastising him for adult heterosexual knowledge and activity. In opening the vessel she brings (the vulva or hymen, Pandora's 'box') the male satisfied his curiosity but sustains the discovery only by punishing himself at the hands of the father god with death and the assorted calamities of postlapsarian life...The myth of the Fall is a highly finished version of the same theme...Sexuality is clearly involved...Róheim points out that the Hebrew verb for 'eat' can also mean coitus ['Eden' in *Psychoanalytic rev.* XXVII 1940; and Theodor Reik *The creation of woman*]...It is impossible to assess how deeply embedded in our consciousness is the Eden legend and how utterly its patterns are planted in our habits of thought. One comes across its tone and design in the most unlikely places, such as Antonioni's film *Blow-Up*...the action...takes place in an idyllic garden, loaded with primal overtones largely sexual, where, prompted by a tempter with a phallic gun, the female again betrays the male to death. The photographer who witnesses the scene reacts as if he were being introduced both to the haggard knowledge of the primal scene [parental coitus] and original sin at the same time.

KATE MILLETT *Sexual politics* Granada 1969

I shall attempt to show that *racism is a sexual phenomenon*. Like sexism in the individual psyche, we can fully understand racism only in terms of the power hierarchies of the family: in the Biblical sense, the races are no more than the various parents and siblings of the Family of Man; and as in the development of sexual classes, the physiological distinction of race became important culturally only due to the unequal distribution of power.

SHULAMITH FIRESTONE *The dialectic of sex: the case for feminist revolution* Granada 1972

I believe that some pollutions are used as analogies for expressing a general view of the social order. For example, there are beliefs that each sex is a danger to the other through contact with sexual fluids. According to other beliefs, only one sex is endangered by contact with the other, usually males from females, but sometimes the reverse. Such patterns of sexual danger can be seen to express sympathy or hierarchy. It is implausible to interpret them as expressing something about the actual relations of the sexes. I suggest that many ideas about sexual dangers are better interpreted as symbols of the relations between parts of society, as mirroring designs of hierarchy or symmetry which apply in the larger social system...The two sexes can serve as a model for the collaboration and distinctiveness of social units...I believe that ideas about separating, purifying, demarcating, and punishing transgressions have as their main function to impose system on an inherently untidy experience. It is only by exaggerating the difference between within and without, above and below, male and female, with and against, that a semblance of order is created...The Lele [a tribe] anxiety about the ritual dangers of sex I attribute to the real disruptive role allotted to sex in their social system. Their men created a status ladder whose successive stages they mounted as they acquired control over more and more women. But they threw the whole system open to competition and so allowed women a double role, as passive pawns, and again as active intriguers...Female pollution in a society of this type is largely related to the attempt to treat women simultaneously as persons and as the currency of male transactions...the story of the Garden of Eden touched a deep chord of sympathy in Lele male breasts. Once told by the missionaries, it was told and retold round pagan hearths with smug relish.

> MARY DOUGLAS *Purity and danger: an analysis of concepts of pollution and taboo* Routledge & Kegan Paul 1966, Penguin 1970, intro and chap 9

Real love between person and person is therefore a relationship in which spirit meets spirit in a dimension in which both the uniformities and the differences of nature, which bind men together and separate them, are transcended...Each soul remains, in a sense, inscrutable to its fellows. It is a possibility only by way of the love of God...a relation between the soul and soul via their common relation to God.

> REINHOLD NIEBUHR *Nature and destiny of man*

Giedion (see above) draws attention to the symbolic function that prehistoric clothing may have had: 'On the front [of a Ukrainian figurine] is a large sexual triangle...Upon the underside of the arching buttocks – the seat of fertility – zigzag or meandering lines have been engraved.' These have been interpreted 'as a symbolical genealogical representation...the starting point for a development of ancestral representations, culminating in the weaving patterns of living primitive peoples. This would strengthen the view that there were prehistoric conceptions of some kind of Magna Mater.'

The cave of dreams and the cave of the dead are the same cave. Ghosts are dreams, and dreams are ghosts: shades, *umbrae*. Sleep is regressive; in dreaming we return to dream time – the age of heroes and ancestors; Roheim's *Eternal Ones of the Dream*; or the primal parents...The basic structure of the dream, the basic dream, is a reaction to being asleep. And 'we can distinguish three stages in this basic dream: (*a*) Sleep is death. (*b*) Sleep is uterine repression. (*c*) Sleep is coitus' [G. R. Levy *The gate of horn* 1948]. The crux is the equation of coming out and going in...Birth is to come out of a womb; and to go into a womb...The birth of the hero is the death of the hero...Both the phallic hero and the female space are made out of the one body of the dreamer. It is then true, after all, that Eve came from Adam's rib, that the separation of the sexes (a fission, divison, duplication) occurs in Adam's sleep, or dream. The Eve that comes from Adam's rib is not just a woman but the Emanation, the world as a woman [Blake *Vision of the last judgement*]...Work is a masturbation dream, punishment for the Fall, which is falling asleep; and also a fall into division of the sexes.

> NORMAN O. BROWN *Love's body* Random House 1966

> We are men formed in Christ's likeness, and we are kept
> like beasts.

That was the declaration of one of the most remarkable organisations of the poor peasants, the Great Society of the fourteenth century. It is not mystifying, but a challenge in terms of a supposedly shared religious belief. Behind much of the feeling of the landless, however, the idea of an earlier and uncorrupted age persisted...It is retrospect as aspiration, for such an idea is drawn not only from the Christian idea of the Garden of Eden – the simple, natural world before the Fall – but also from a version of the Golden Age which is more than that of a magically self-yielding nature. This version is based on the idea of a primitive community, a primitive communism. This is not in Hesiod, where the men of the Golden Age live like gods. Its origins seem to be Hellenistic, and it is explicit in Virgil:

> no peasants subdued the fields; it was not lawful even to assign or divide the ground with landmarks: men sought the common gain, and the earth itself bore everything more generously at no one's bidding.
>
> (*Georgics*, 1)

This is a fusion of ideas of the self-yielding earth and a conscious community of property and purpose...this must be distinguished from the asocial and mystified Golden Age of the lordly uses: the self-yielding earth ratified by its proprietor, its Lord...In the words of the Great Society: 'All things under Heaven ought to be common.' It was a claim that was to be continued through the seventeenth-century Diggers to the Land Chartists and the radical labourers of our own time. The happier past was almost desperately insisted upon, but as an impulse to change rather than to ratify the actual inheritance.

RAYMOND WILLIAMS *The country and the city* Chatto & Windus 1973

Christopher Columbus did not doubt that he had come near the Earthly Paradise. He believed that the fresh water currents he encountered in the Gulf of Paria originated in the four rivers of the Garden of Eden...The colonisation of the two Americas began under an eschatalogical sign: people believed that the time had come to renew the Christian world, and the true renewal was the return to the Earthly Paradise or, at the very least, the beginning again of sacred history, the reiteration of the prodigious events spoken of in the Bible.

> MIRCEA ELIADE *The quest: history and meaning in religion* Chicago U.P. 1939 chap 6 'Paradise and Utopia: mythical geography and eschatology'

Myths are the most accurate means that the human mind has devised of representing its own immeasurably complex structure and content... This great pastoral inheritance, the legacy of Theocritus and Virgil, satisfying an ideal of harmony and repose, embracing a wealth of unexacting beauty and delight, is exemplified by such fantasies...as the Cologne *Paradise-Garden*, and Spenser's Garden of Adonis in *The Faerie Queene*...As an image, the ideal garden perennially beguiles us with its promise of secure happiness and ordered harmony; but to the indefinite *occupation* of gardens, not to speak of their care and maintenance, there attaches a quite exceptional degree of tedium and restlessness. The most tactful poetic solution is to treat it as an unrealized possibility, a place which we are just on the point of occupying or which we might have occupied:

> Footfalls echo in the memory
> Down the passage which we did not take
> Towards the door we never opened
> Into the rose-garden   [ELIOT *Burnt Norton*]

Coleridge represents Kubla Khan as decreeing and paying out his pleasure-garden, but not as entering it. Milton, otherwise constrained by his source and epic purpose, embodies in his construction at every level the imaginative principle which must subvert it. His splendid baroque paradise, stately, verdurous, diversified with noble rivers, the epitome of the sure dispensation, would have been totally uncompelling without the satanic assault...the earthly paradise is insufficient for man because it is incapable of uniting the opposed ideals symbolized by snake [unpredictable] and tree [stable]...Over against it, as we have seen, stands a more severe paradisial myth...reaching back to the unknown first time when the snake-encircled tree was incorporated in the ideal enclave, not as earthly elysium but as divine precinct, to set forth a reconciliation of these divergent human ends, and the power of the imagination by which it may be accomplished...to frequent the region of the infinitely various, to stand rooted in a continuing order.

JOHN ARMSTRONG *The paradise myth* Oxford U.P. 1969

...every civilization has to exact labor time for the procurement of the necessities and luxuries of life. But not every kind and mode of labor is essentially irreconcilable with the pleasure principle. The human relations connected with work may 'provide for a very considerable discharge of libidinal component impulses, narcissistic, aggressive, and even erotic' [Freud *Civilization and its discontents*]...The irreconcilable conflict is not between work (reality principle) and Eros (pleasure principle), but between *alienated* labor (performance principle) and Eros. The notion of non-alienated, libidinal work will be discussed below...In psychoanalytical literature, the development of libidinal work relations is... considered as a feature of primitive societies rather than as a possibility of mature civilizations...

To the Arapesh, the world is a garden that must be tilled, not for one's self, not in pride and boasting, not for hoarding and usury, but that the yams and the dogs and the pigs and most of all the children may grow ...[hence] the lack of conflict between the old and the young...the emphasis upon co-operation.

[Margaret Mead *Sex and temperament in three primitive societies* Smith n.d.]

...nature is taken, not as an object of domination and exploitation, but as a 'garden' which can grow while making human beings grow. It is the attitude that experiences man and nature as joined in a non-repressive and still functioning order...Certainly there can be 'pleasure' in alienated labor too...all may feel pleasure in a 'job well done'. However, either this pleasure is extraneous (anticipation of reward), or it is the satisfaction (itself a token of repression) of being well occupied, in the right place, of contributing one's part to the functioning of the apparatus...such pleasure has nothing to do with primary instinctual gratification.

HERBERT MARCUSE *Eros and civilization: a philosophical inquiry into Freud* Routledge & Kegan Paul 1956 chaps 2...10

See also *Song of Solomon*; Ovid *Metamorphoses* (trans. Horace Gregory) v 385 (fields of Enna); Spenser *FQ* III vi (Garden of Adonis); Donne *Twickenham Garden* (an anti-paradise of despair);

Marvell *Bermudas* (an actual 17c paradise for political refugees) and *The garden* (only one sex); gardens in *Four quartets*, especially *Burnt Norton*; William Morris *The earthly paradise* and various other country house and garden poems cited, for example, under Jonson in Broadbent *Poets of the 17c* 1974 vol I. Specialized study might start from material cited by Aers and Radzinowicz ed. *PL* VII–VIII in this series; Henri Baudet *Paradise on earth: some thoughts on European images of non-European man* trans. Elizabeth Wentholt 1965; material cited in Broadbent *Some graver subject* 1960 (especially theologians and travel writers) and *PL: introduction* in this series; R. R. Cawley *M and the literature of travel* Princeton 1951; Valerie Carnes 'Time and language in M's *PL*' *English literary history* XXXVII 1970; E. R. Curtius *European literature and the Latin Middle Ages* 1948 trans. 1953; Joseph E. Duncan *M's earthly paradise: a historical study of Eden* Minneapolis 1972 (University of Minnesota monographs in the humanities 5); J. Martin Evans *PL and the Genesis tradition* 1968 and works cited in the 'Topics: Book IX' section of his ed. *PL* IX–X in this series; David Evett '"Paradice's only map": the *topos* of the *locus amoenus* and the structure of Marvell's *Upon Appleton House*' *Publications of the Modern Language Association* LXXXV 1970; A. Bartlett Giametti *The earthly paradise and the renaissance epic* Princeton 1966; Harry Levin *The myth of the Golden Age in the renaissance* 1970; Barbara Lewalski 'Innocence and experience in M's Eden' in *New essays on PL* ed. Thomas Kranidas, Berkeley 1971; Arthur O. Lovejoy and George Boas *A documentary history of primitivism and related ideas* Baltimore 1935; Jeffry B. Spencer *Heroic nature: ideal landscape in English poetry from Marvell to Thomson* Evanston 1973; Stanley N. Stewart *The enclosed garden: the tradition and the image in 17c poetry* 1966; Edward William Tayler *Nature and art in renaissance literature* 1964; and of course the works cited in this volume.

Addenda to resources for PL

This volume completes the editing of *PL* in this series which began in 1972 so here is a highly selective list of recent works on the poem not yet cited in the Cambridge Milton (August 1975).

ASIMOV, ISAAC *Asimov's annotated PL* 1974. Includes *PR*.

BENSTOCK, BERNARD 'Exiles: "Paradox Lust" and "Lost Pala-days"' *English literary history* XXXVI 1969 739–56. Reminds us of Joyce's use of Milton in his play and in *Finnegan's wake*.

CAREY, JOHN *Milton* 1969. Literature in perspective series.

CURRAN, STUART and JOSEPH WITTREICH ed. *Blake's sublime allegory: essays on 'The Four Zoas', 'Milton' and 'Jerusalem'* Madison 1973.

FISH, STANLEY E. *Surprised by sin: the reader in PL* 1967.

GREEN, THOMAS 'The norms of epic' in *Perspectives on poetry* ed. J. L. Calderwood and H. E. Toliver 1968.

HARTMAN, GEOFFREY 'Adam on the grass with balsamum' *English literary history* XXXVI 1969 (vol. contains other articles on M). Reply by R. M. Adams 'Contra Hartman' in *17c imagery: essays on uses of figurative language from Donne to Farquhar* ed. Earl Miner 1971.

HILL, CHRISTOPHER 'M the radical' *Times literary supplement* 29 Nov 74 pp. 1330–2.

HUCKABY, CALVIN *JM: an annotated bibliography 1929–1968* Pittsburgh 1969.

LEHNER, ERNST and JOANNAH *Devils, demons, death and damnation* Dover pictorial archives 1971. (Recent attention to Odilon Redon – eg his painting of *A fallen angel* – and other French symbolists has brought other material to view.)

MACCULLUM, H. R. 'M and sacred history: Books XI and XII of *PL*' in *Essays in English literature from the renaissance to the Victorian age. Presented to A. S. P. Woodhouse* ed. M. McClure and F. W. Watt Toronto 1964.

RAJAN, BALACHANDRA *The lofty rhyme* 1970.

SMITH, ERIC *Some versions of the fall: the myth of the fall of man in English literature* 1973.

STEADMAN, JOHN M. *M's epic characters: image and idol* Chapel Hill 1968.

WEDGWOOD, C. V. *M and his world* 1969. Picture book, cf Wolfe below.

WHEELER, THOMAS *PL and the modern reader* Athens, Georgia 1974.

WOLFE, DON M. *M and his England* Princeton 1971. Splendidly illustrated; cf Wedgwood above.

We should have mentioned the opera *Milton* by Gasparo Spontini 1774–1851. An adaptation of *PL* by Karoly Kazimir was performed at the Thalia Theatre, Budapest, in July 1970 and another by Gordon Honeycombe at the Theatre Royal, York, in November 1974 (with Gielgud as M) as part of the tercentenary of M's death. It was also celebrated on radio, at Chalfont St Giles and more extensively in the States.